CHANGING
HATS

WHILE MANAGING CHANGE

FROM

SOCIAL WORK

PRACTICE TO

ADMINISTRATION

FELICE DAVIDSON PERLMUTTER
and
WENDY P. CROOK

P9-DBI-998

National Association of Social Workers
Washington, DC

Gary Bailey, MSW, President
Elizabeth J. Clark, PhD, ACSW, MPH, Executive Director

NASW PRESS

Cheryl Y. Bradley, *Publisher*
Paula L. Delo, *Executive Editor*
Heather Brady, *Editor*
Leonard Rosenbaum, *Indexer*
Robin Bourjaily, *Proofreader*

Cover by Eye to Eye Design Studios
Interior design by Electronic Quill
Printed and bound by Port City Press

Library of Congress Cataloging-in-Publication Data

Perlmutter, Felice Davidson, 1931–
    Changing hats while managing change : from social work practice to administration / Felice Davidson Perlmutter and Wendy P. Crook.—2nd ed.
        p.   cm.
    Includes bibliographical references and index.
    ISBN 0-87101-361-4
1. Social work administration. I. Crook, Wendy P. II. Title.
    HV41.P453   2004
    361.3'068'4—dc22   2004006886

Printed in the United States of America

Contents

Preface and Acknowledgments

Many of you may ask yourselves this question: "Do I want to become a social work administrator?" You wonder whether you would enjoy a change of role and whether you would be effective in that change of role. This is a natural concern, given that you entered the field of social work to work directly with clients, and your graduate education prepared you for direct practice.

Yet the field is changing and new opportunities are arising. You have been working for several years in your agency, and you are ready for a change. It is not surprising that the route to advancement you are considering is that of administration.

You should know that the practice of administration in social work is the most recently developed specialization in the profession. As the field developed, and as agencies became larger and more complex, it became clear that it was no longer appropriate for social workers to go up the ladder from frontline practice to supervision or middle management and, ultimately, to executive roles without preparation for these new functions. A change from direct practice to administration requires new personal orientations and new conceptual and technical information.

However, until relatively recently there has been little available in the literature or even in professional master's degree programs that could help students understand what administration is about or help them decide whether administration is the professional route they wish to take.

Changing Hats, when published in 1990, was one of the first professional social work books to focus on social work administration. The book had two target populations. First, it was intended as a resource for a broad audience of social work practitioners who were unfamiliar with the administrator's role but who were exploring their own inclinations to move into this new arena. Second, it was designed to serve as a textbook for students in direct-practice social work programs who should understand administration not only in terms of its relationship to enhancing service delivery but also as an important social work method.

Many books have been written about social work administration since that first edition of *Changing Hats* was published. Those books differ from *Changing Hats* in that they are technical in nature, designed to help professionals who are already in the administrative positions perform their roles more effectively.

This new edition of *Changing Hats* has retained its original purpose: to help practitioners determine whether they wish to shift their careers from direct practice to administrative practice as well as to educate social work students about administrative practice. It also can help those social workers who have moved up the ladder without administrative training to understand their new challenges. Its language is nontechnical, and the extensive use of case material is designed to provide a direct and accessible linkage to real-life situations.

The content of this volume is selective, as it stems from and reflects the authors' work and interests as both teachers and researchers. It is based largely on our lectures, consultations, and publications. The individual chapters highlight theoretical and conceptual content and address some of the technical areas of administration in a descriptive manner that is intended to inform the reader about the subject.

This volume is organized as follows. Part I focuses on the more abstract and contextual aspects of social work administration. The chapters examine the personal, systems, and organizational dimensions of administrative social work practice.

Part II addresses an array of administrative roles that reflect contemporary realities in the field. The discussion is applications oriented and makes extensive use of case material. The reader should feel free to use his or her own experience and organizational setting as case material on which to test the theoretical orientations discussed in this volume.

Part III shifts the discussion to the most fundamental underpinnings of the profession, the ethics of the social work profession. It links the direct practitioner with the administrator, as all share these common precepts.

Changing Hats will meet its objective if it helps its readers clarify their career directions. For those who choose to embark on a career in administration there is a vast amount of literature to be explored, whether it be in formal educational settings or through independent study. This further exploration is essential for providing a broader and deeper understanding of social administration in particular and administration and management in general.

We wish to acknowledge the work of our colleagues and of social service agencies as they serve the complex needs of a broad array of citizens in need of diverse services. These are not easy times, as social problems have become more complex and as social resources devoted to meeting these problems are in shorter supply. The case material in this volume reflects some of the realities of work in the field.

PART I

*THEORETICAL
PERSPECTIVES*

Chapter 1

Introducing the Discussion

Changing Hats while Managing Change was deliberately chosen as the title for this book because it projects an image of proactive leadership, as this book focuses on the proactive practitioner who is moving into the administrative role. Social work practitioners must understand new expectations and develop new skills before they don an administrator's hat. Consequently, this first chapter is devoted to answering the immediate, and perhaps the most obvious, questions.

What Is Unique about Social Work Administration?

Social work practitioners have been drawn to the field because they are interested in working with people who are seeking to improve their lives. The client may be a widower with three children who seeks personal service on a one-to-one basis, a group composed of parents of gay children seeking support and help in accepting this reality, or a larger group, such as a neighborhood that has a large proportion of community-based housing for individuals in the mental health system and that is seeking to ensure neighborhood stability. The unifying thread that runs across all these examples is change—of individuals, groups, or communities—through direct contact between the social worker and the client-consumer.

Among the many ways by which social workers enter the field, there are three primary routes. Some have clearly selected social work for their professional career and have completed their master's of social work (MSW) degree; others have chosen social work as their undergraduate major and have earned a bachelor's of social work (BSW) degree. Yet others have entered the field by chance because of the availability of a job, although their undergraduate degree is either in a related discipline (for example, psychology, sociology, or urban studies) or even in an unrelated discipline (for example, literature or history).

Although most practitioners enjoy their direct-service roles and seek to improve their repertoire of skills through continuing education in areas such as family therapy, clinical supervision, or community work, some are attracted to administration. In fact, many practitioners have opportunities within their agencies for promotion to administrative positions, and indeed, most supervisors in social work agencies began their careers as direct practitioners. These groups—those who are attracted to administrative practice and those who are presented with career choices involving promotion to administrative jobs—often think they are uninformed and feel insecure about making this change.

Social work practitioners often raise questions that illustrate these doubts. What do administrators do? Do I have the personality or style to be an administrator? Can I shift from direct practice to administration? Can I be an administrator if I am not experienced in financial matters? What does it mean to "manage change"?

This book is designed to help practitioners and aspiring social work administrators who have these questions explore the ins and outs of social work administration, with an emphasis on the management of professional and organizational change. It focuses on critical dimensions of administrative practice and seeks to broaden the reader's understanding of this specialization. It should help the reader come to an informed decision concerning the following question: Should I become a social work administrator?

In this book, we focus on both upper and middle management levels of administration, the levels at which most organizational change is initiated and managed. The theoretical underpinnings and the necessary skills are dramatically different from those needed for direct practice and serve to introduce readers to unfamiliar areas. Because most professionals enter administration through middle management, we devote a chapter to the unique roles of middle managers.

It is important to present working definitions of the central concepts of the book: social work administration and change management. For the purposes of this volume, *social work administration* refers to leadership and management activities in social service agencies, both public and private, which make possible the effective and efficient provision of services to client populations. This takes place by translating social policies and agency policies into social programs.

Change management refers to leadership and management activities aimed at assessing the need for change, planning and promoting change, developing a change-friendly environment, and evaluating the success of change efforts to meet new needs in a changing environment. In effect, the role of administrator includes that of change agent. The close relationship between these central concepts should be apparent to the reader, as effective social work administration requires effective change management and vice versa.

The term *administrator* means the administrative practitioner who performs macro-level social work with responsibility for the well-being of a multitude of constituents: clients, staff, volunteers, board of directors, the agency as a whole, and even the broader public.

Change management takes place in agencies that can be direct service or administrative planning, be it in the nonprofit, for-profit, or public sectors. Because the focus here is on the generic elements of administrative practice, these organizational settings will be referred to interchangeably.

What Are the Assumptions that Underpin this Discussion?

An understanding of the underlying assumptions, biases, and preferences that inform this book will enrich our discussion of social work administration. These starting points are important for determining the approach to the material and will help the reader read and digest the content critically.

1. Social Work Experience Is Valuable. The first assumption that underpins the discussion in this volume is that the route to social work administration is best traveled from the starting point of direct practice or experience in social service. Because of their knowledge of programs, clients, and service systems, "social workers are the preferred leadership for human service organizations" (Rapp & Poertner, 1992, p. 11). This is counter to the view that training in management through a master of business administration (MBA) degree can most effectively and efficiently provide managerial leadership for all organizations. As social service organizations have grown in response to increased government contracting, boards of directors are often tempted to hire administrators with business backgrounds to manage social welfare agencies and their burgeoning budgets. However, we believe that a social work background (ideally, experience plus education) is key to successful social work administration.

The perspectives gained by working as a direct practitioner provide the administrator with an invaluable base for responsive and effective agency leadership. However, specialized education in social work administration is important, because it provides the appropriate theoretical, analytical, and technical skills necessary for performing the broad array of administrative roles, including a knowledge base related to consumer needs (Slavin, 1980).

2. The Administrator Is a Change Agent. The second assumption that underpins this discussion is that the role of the social work administrator is a proactive one, a role that provides leadership in the broadest sense. Not only is it necessary to keep the shop running smoothly and efficiently to meet current needs, but it is also necessary to have vision, to anticipate what is possible and necessary for tomorrow. In his classic volume *Leadership in Administration,* Selznick (1957) articulates this viewpoint beautifully:

> If one of the great functions of administration is the exertion of cohesive force in the direction of institutional security, another great function is the creation of conditions that will make possible

in the future what is excluded in the present. This requires a strategy of change that looks to the attainment of new capabilities more nearly fulfilling the truly felt needs and aspirations of the institution. (pp. 153–154)

Nearly half a century after Selznick's observation was made we recognize the centrality of the administrator as change agent, a role not reserved for social work administration alone but implicit in all administrative practice.

3. *The Administrator Is an Advocate.* The third assumption, which is directly related to the principle of proactive leadership, is that social work administrators must serve as advocates for the constituency they serve. This entails an ongoing commitment not only to informing the broader society about the characteristics and needs of their clientele but also demanding better social policies and more resources on their behalf. Our professional *Code of Ethics* states the following: "Social workers should advocate within and outside their agencies for adequate resources to meet clients' needs" (NASW, 1999, 3.07). In fact, as early as 1969, an Ad Hoc Committee on Advocacy was appointed by the NASW to address this special obligation, and it issued a report stating that the social work administrator "is bound to act as an advocate on behalf of clients under his jurisdiction" (Ad Hoc Committee on Advocacy, 1969, p.18).

And yet, although advocacy is generally recognized as an essential element of the social work profession, it remains an ideal to be achieved, as it is all too often neglected when social work administrators are caught up in responding to countless immediate pressures. A national study of family agency social work executives found that in spite of their social work values, advocacy was low on their list of priorities (Perlmutter & Adams, 1994).

This does not mean that administrative advocacy is simple to achieve or is without risks. But it is important to note that all organizations are stimulated to change when risk taking and advocacy permeate their agendas. In our view, administrative advocacy is often a distinguishing characteristic of social work administration.

4. Administrators Are Responsible for Empowerment. The fourth assumption, which is related to advocacy, is that the empowerment of staff and client-consumers is an administrative responsibility. Given the enormous pressures faced by administrators, it is often simpler to yield to the temptation to take charge, to make decisions without input from those affected by the outcomes of the decisions, or to go it alone. This runs counter to the well-established social work value of client self-determination, which is succinctly stated in the *Code of Ethics:* "Social workers respect and promote the right of clients to self-determination and assist clients in their efforts to identify and clarify their goals" (NASW, 1999, 1.02).

The administrator who is working with highly trained professionals must duly heed the professional concern with and acceptance of the value of self-determination. The challenge is one of translating beliefs into practice. The concept of empowerment flows directly from this professional requisite, and it is the responsibility of the administrative practitioner to broaden this focus on the client to include all levels of staff. The notion of administrative responsibility for staff and client empowerment is another unique and distinguishing characteristic of social work administration.

These four assumptions should be kept in mind. The ideal social work administrator is a change agent and an advocate who is experienced and is dedicated to staff empowerment. This administrator can deal with the various issues and dilemmas encountered in the practice of social work administration and is the actor who will be discussed in this volume. In fact, the unique identity of social work administration may flow from these assumptions and may well serve to answer this question: How is social work administration different from management in general?

What Is the Thrust of this Book? Why Focus on Theory?

The ability to understand theory and to be able to apply it provides the social work administrator with great flexibility. This book will present selected theoretical concepts throughout that are important for administration and will illustrate them with case materials from a variety of

TABLE 1-1.
Primary Activities for Social Work Practitioners

Social work practice level	Primary activities
Direct care worker	• Assess and allocate resource needs of clients • Coordinate client activities • Implement procedures
Middle manager	• Assess and allocate resource needs of staff • Coordinate staff activities • Develop procedures
Administrator	• Assess, obtain, and allocate resource needs of programs • Coordinate program activities • Develop policies

social work settings. Whereas some of the material is generic and is applicable across all settings, other portions are specific to a particular situation and were selected to highlight a particular concept.

Throughout the book we provide tables that extract key concepts from the narrative. For example, Table 1-1 shows the basic differences in activities for direct, supervisory, and administrative practitioners in social work organizations.

We will return to this table later in the book and develop others that similarly highlight key concepts.

This volume focuses on both theory and practice, because theory informs practice. Not only does it open the door to a consideration of new vistas, but it also creates the opportunity for creative choice and provides the social work administrator with a wide range of options for effective practice.

A Note about Theory

Professions are governed by general principles, or theories, that serve as guides for practitioners in the plying of their craft. Social work administrators must be schooled in the theories that interpret and explain the events in the domain before they can develop innovative and effective solutions. Although it is true that creativity and individual styles are important, administrators have at stake the personal, social, and economic well-being of their client systems. Thus, although individual style and creativity can give form and substance to the administrator's role, it is the theoretical base of tested ideas from which he or she draws that underpins responsible performance.

Social workers are aware of and are informed about the various theories that create a framework for their work. Social work direct practitioners may draw from one or more of the major psychological theories (for example, psychoanalytic, behavioral, and humanistic), and they may use various practice models in a wide range of settings. Practitioners are increasingly shifting their approaches and adding new treatment models, such as solution focused (de Shazer, 1991), crisis intervention (Golan, 1978; Rapoport, 1970), task centered (Epstein & Brown, 2002), and family systems (Lindblad-Goldberg, Dore, & Stern, 1998; Minuchin, 1974).

Community practitioners can make selections from recent approaches to community change, such as the systems model (Kettner, Daley, & Nichols, 1985) and PREPARE, a framework for assessing community change potential (Kirst-Ashman & Gull, 1997).

Organization theory, stimulated by the early writings of Parsons (1961), Emery & Trist (1969), Selznick (1957), and the later work of Hasenfeld (1983), Neugeboren (1985), and Powell & Friedken (1987), has provided an important perspective for social administration. In addition, although much of social work administrative practice has drawn its theoretical base from business organizations, in recent years practice principles for human service managers have been developed from their own field. Examples include the human relations perspective, contingency theory, political economy perspective, ecological perspective, institutional perspective, and feminist models (Hasenfeld, 2000).

We can highlight the benefits of a theoretical framework that can serve as a guide for the social work administrator. Administration is a complex process that requires constant decision making on a broad array of problems; it is tempting, and not unusual, to make these decisions on an ad hoc basis to meet immediate needs and thereby to reduce pressure. A theoretical model helps the administrator redefine the problem and formulate a solution that is appropriate for the organization. In all cases, regardless of the field, the administrator should not work only from an idiosyncratic, or gut, sense; the work should also reflect an approach that has been tested in the broader community of ideas. A theory provides guidelines for professional analysis and action.

Theory serves another crucial function. It is very easy for beleaguered executives to personalize the problems they are dealing with and to experience personal discomfort.

Mr. Stone was the CEO of a major mental health facility. He prided himself on his relationships with his staff and on knowing everyone's name and family situation.

When the staff decided to unionize he took it personally as a hostile act and was extremely agitated, unable to handle the situation professionally. A consultation with an outside colleague who gave him some material to read about conflict theory, leadership theories, and labor relations provided him with a perspective to appropriately deal with this new situation.

This example illustrates that a theoretical awareness helps the administrator to generalize the analysis, to depersonalize the process, and to view the problem as an expected and universal occurrence.

In any discussion of theory, however, it is important to point out that although theory seeks to explain behavior, it is not the same as a scientifically proven law. With this proviso, note that the practitioner is operating in a flexible context and has the freedom to choose that which seems appropriate and useful. For example, in social work administration there is often an assumption that participatory democracy, an element of human relations theory, should be the basis for decision making in the social service agency. Although this theory may be compatible with social work values, its utilization must be understood in relation to the specific organizational setting (that is, it can work "only in certain situations involving certain staff and certain managers" [Weinbach, 1990, p. 68]).

A slavish adherence to theory is a foolish consistency, but the external perspective provided by theory can create the possibility of a more liberated and flexible leadership. The social work profession continues to consider the merits of theory as a basis for practice and research. Whereas Thyer (2001) believes that "so much of practice itself is not theoretically driven" (p. 15), Gomory (2001) asserts that to determine the efficacy of a treatment, social workers must perform "a review of what theoretical notions organize the intervention" (p. 40).

A Final Word

Contemplating a career in social work administration is exciting. For some social workers, the possibility of providing better services to clients by helping to make the agency work more effectively and efficiently is challenging. For others the prospect of entering into a new, yet not entirely different, arena while learning new theory and skills is equally challenging.

Of course, there are different strokes for different folks. The trick is to discover which route maximizes personal preference and satisfaction, attributes that are essential to being effective professionally.

This volume will expose the reader to new ways of thinking, different theoretical perspectives, and new methodologies and technologies as well as administrative challenges and methods of problem solving. It should soon be clear to the reader whether this material is relevant to her or his particular situation. If it is, the reader stands ready to contemplate new career directions in the field of social work.

The Context of
Social Work Administration

As a social work method, social work administration operates within the external societal and internal professional contexts. The administrator is the bridge between the two and must be sensitive and responsive to both. This chapter sets the stage for an understanding of the role of proactive leadership in creating the changes that are necessary in an ever-changing context.

The Societal Context

Our society is experiencing an era of dramatic social change that will result in increasing demands for social service provisions. According to Austin (2000), these include

> longer life spans; cultural diversity and the assimilation of newcomers into the society of the United States; realignment of the position of women; changes in the structure of the family and discontinuities in the growing-up experiences of children and adolescents; the management of chronic illness conditions, including mental illness, through medications; the combination of economic opportunity and economic turmoil resulting from the globalization of economy; the impact of new technologies; and the persistence of economic inequality. (p. 49)

An understanding of some of the major changes that affect the human services is essential to understanding the proactive leadership role of the human service executive, including an understanding of the turbulent environment, our changing value system, the changing technology, for-profit organizations, and equal opportunity practices.

The Turbulent Environment

In an early paper that is a classic in the organizational literature, Emery and Trist (1969) identified the environment of an organization as being critical to an understanding of its behavior, because not only the organization but also the environment in which it is embedded are in constant flux. Their theoretical formulation accurately predicted our current reality.

Emery and Trist conceptualized four types of environments, ranging from placid and relatively unchanging to dynamic. Of importance to our discussion of the context of human service administration is the type 4 environment, which is identified as one of turbulence accompanied by areas of relative uncertainty. There is a "deepening interdependence between the economic and other facets of the society.... Economic organizations are increasingly enmeshed in legislation and public regulation. . . . There is an increasing reliance on research and development to achieve the capacity to meet competitive challenge" (Emery & Trist, 1969, p. 249).

Our society is currently experiencing a type 4 turbulent environment, which was certainly not always the case in the development of social welfare programs in the 20th century (Lieby, 1987). That the social work administrator is dramatically affected by this turbulence is illustrated in a poignant letter, written after government contracting became a dominant factor for human service programs. The pressures of writing proposals and accountability were a new phenomenon:

> As you may know, I came into administration like most executives of my vintage—through the skill of being a pretty good practitioner and then a good supervisor. . . . Fortunately, I did come into the job as executive ... when there was still the usual

rhythm of going on year to year, and changes, if they occurred, took about 2 to 4 years and you had a lot of time to get used to them. I don't believe that there is any place in the country that such a rhythm is possible, today at least, if one is going to survive. (Personal correspondence)

Thus, "the expansion of the number and scope of categorical federal social welfare programs brought increased attention to the preparation of social welfare managers" (Austin, 2000, p. 39). Yet compared with today's pressures, even that decade seems placid.

The Changing Value System

A major source of the background turbulence in U.S. society is the dramatic shift in the value system that supports social services. The fact that every four to eight years a new president and every two years a new U. S. Congress can completely reverse the intent of their predecessors creates great pressures and tensions in the social service system. One need only look at welfare reform; at managed care; and at the decimation of the poverty program, community legal services, community mental health, and housing and urban development, to recognize that the cost of political change is great. Although it might be argued that (1) negative perceptions of the welfare system in the United States have remained relatively stable over time and (2) social policy shifts have been largely incremental, the ebb and flow of public acceptance and support require social administrators to constantly adapt to changing expectations.

The rate of change in the public mandate is great, but of even greater significance is the change in the public mood in terms of social policies and programs. In a provocative paper, Stern (1984) argued that these shifts are predictable and that the American people are basically conservative and unwilling to commit themselves to a welfare state ideology : "Thus, political capitalism's legacy is not based, as is social democracy's, on a critique of capitalism. Rather, it attempts to make minor corrections in a social system that is assumed 'naturally' to work well" (p. 5).

Although the conflict in values and the political shifts experienced on a regular basis affect all of the helping professions, social welfare programs are most vulnerable because they are the direct products of the social philosophy and fiscal policies of federal, state, and local governments. Social welfare administrators will need to develop innovative strategies for professional and organizational survival because

> the increasing conservatism of national political power can be expected to give added impetus to control of the size, scope, and cost of government; the predilection for private-sector and free-market solutions to economic and social problems; and the preference for state, local, and community control over public policy in general and social welfare policy in particular. (Martin, 2000, p. 58)

The proactive leadership and advocacy approaches discussed in Chapter 1 are of particular importance for social work administrators as they struggle to survive in this type 4 environment and ensure that clients' needs are being met. In the proactive leadership role the administrator ensures that changes within the organization as it adapts to the turbulent environment are consistent with the agency goals and mission. The administrator as advocate works to educate the public about emerging and worsening social problems.

A case example illustrates the effect of ideology on administrative choices and describes a reactive, rather than a proactive, administrator.

A nationally renowned and respected social work administrator who was employed in a very prestigious private social service agency convinced the board of directors to shift agency priorities from serving Medicaid-eligible patients to serving middle-class, insured populations who could generate third-party payments. When asked what would happen to the poor who needed the agency's service, the response was: "I can't carry them on my back."

In the quest for efficiency, as reflected by the financial balance, the agency's effectiveness was lost and the administrator unwittingly described the details of the destruction of the integrity of the agency, its mandate, and its mission. Clearly, this was not an easy matter. However, a social work administrator using an advocacy perspective might have sought different resources to ensure that the needs of the agency's target population received the services it needed. In the role of change agent the administrator also might have convinced the board of directors to take into consideration the effect of its decision on the agency's traditional client base.

The value framework that underpins administrative decision making is a critical one, comparable with the value framework that informs the mission of the agency. In this case, both were misplaced when the administrator did not address the adverse effects of the decision on the agency's original clientele. The result can be characterized as goal displacement, wherein the means displace the ends and the agency drifts from its mission (Neugeboren, 1991).

Changing Technology

The rapidly changing technology witnessed in recent decades is another factor that should be considered by those in administrative practice. The nature of administration in all sectors has been changed dramatically with the advent of computers. Computers have taken over many functions, and although the benefits are great, Zimmerman and Broughton (1999) point out that "these developments are likely to have a profound effect on how nonprofit organizations function and how their staff and clients or patrons interact" (p. 326). Almost all social welfare initiatives depend upon access to useful information about services and clients (Schoech, 2000). Moreover, "because of the complexity of social welfare agencies and their environments, the task of managing their information resources is more difficult than the same task in business" (p. 321).

Zimmerman and Broughton (1999) identified several ways in which social work administrators have had to adapt to the rapidly changing technology in their agencies: "Find ways to fund it, manage it, anticipate changes caused by it and, often most daunting, try to anticipate the direction of the next technological advance" (p. 325). Here the proactive leadership role of the social work administrator is key, with many difficult decisions confronting him or her.

To aid in the decision-making processes associated with the management of technological change, Schoech (2000) developed an eight-stage technology development process. The human services executive needs to understand the process and determine how it should be managed. Initially, it is important to evaluate feasibility and preparedness within the organization, which should include a review of the agency's mission and goals for congruence with the technology effort. The administrator then performs an assessment of the current capacities and information needs in the agency. The planning process proceeds to conceptual design and detailed design and development to identify specific hardware, software, and system needs. The next stage, testing and preparation, is key to smooth initiation of the technology system and should involve all staff training activities as well as opportunities for staff to provide feedback. The final two stages are monitoring and evaluation; and operation, maintenance, and modification; these are critical for ongoing effectiveness of the technology system

In an early paper on the topic, Wilson (1980) raised challenging questions regarding the compatibility of the new technology with social work administrators' value systems and responsibilities for advocacy. He feared that the consumer's interests would be sacrificed for bureaucratic interests. More recently, Schoech (2000) cautioned against ignoring ethical issues related to the sharing of client data among agencies through technology. These concerns include privacy, confidentiality, and informed consent. The challenge for social work administrators is to manage the transition to a technologically enhanced agency while advocating for the needs and rights of clients as well as staff.

For-Profit Organizations

Although little is currently known about the differences between nonprofit and for-profit social work organizations in terms of client and staff outcomes, the growing trend of the for-profit sector's involvement in social welfare cannot be ignored as a context for the social work administrator. The attraction of the for-profit sector for governmental funders originated in the belief that intractable social problems needed alternative service delivery systems, with competition seen as the means to efficiency and effectiveness (Gibelman, 2000). In the last decade we have seen entire state welfare systems, child protection organizations, health care providers, and others either arise as or convert to for-profit status to maximize their ability to win competitive contracts with government agencies.

This trend shows no signs of reversing, which means that social workers increasingly will be providing services in for-profit organizations. The challenge for the social work administrator in the environmental context of increased competition and profitization is to ensure that the organizational goals of profit-making enterprises do not supplant those of client benefit. What does the administrator do when third-party payments do not cover the cost of care that clients have requested and need? How can social workers accurately assess the needs of their clients when choices are limited to those services that are profitable? How does the social worker whose job is already complex survive in a competitive environment? How can the social worker ethically respond to directives for "creaming" (that is, admitting only those clients who are easy to serve and therefore cost less than others)? Because of a concern for "a potential decline in the quality of care" (Gibelman, 2000, p. 129), we consider this trend in using for-profits to deliver human services a potential threat to the well-being of social welfare clients.

These and other concerns must be addressed by the social work administrator, who must balance the need of the agency to produce profits for its owners with the needs of clients to successfully attain their goals. Thus, in the role of advocate the administrator ensures that clients who seek help get it and that workers get the resources and support they need. In the proactive role the administrator in a for-profit setting develops innovative agency structures and processes to ensure that the multiple goals of the organization are met.

Equal Opportunity Practices

Another factor for consideration arises from the observation that human resources in social service also are undergoing many changes related to the external environment. Iglehart (2000) comments on the benefits of workforce diversity: "In an environment marked by continuous change, the organization's resiliency, adaptability, viability, and flexibility are increased through workforce diversity" (p. 427). Administrators are responsible for developing and acting from a diversity practice perspective. The topic of human resources is a broad one and can include, among other topics, personnel administration, employee motivation, and remuneration and benefits.

The discussion here focuses on the increasing presence and new consciousness concerning women and minorities in management. These issues are addressed separately to highlight their particular concerns.

Social work has traditionally been identified as a female-dominated profession. Yet the data show that despite the feminist movement, the proportion of females in social work administration has actually declined over the last two decades (Bargal, 2000). This may be because of budgetary cutbacks and their resultant layoffs or may reflect a bias against women in management (Bargal, 2000). Female administrators earn significantly lower salaries than do their male counterparts (Koeske & Koeske, 2000). Chernesky (1998) identifies the problem of organizational and attitudinal barriers which prevent women from achieving upward mobility within social welfare organizations. These barriers result in a disproportionate representation of men in higher-paying managerial positions.

Although much attention has been given to the attitudes and behaviors of females who wish to succeed in administration, emphasis has been placed on career development through courses focused on assertiveness training and conquering the fear of success. This approach has only served to perpetuate a stereotype of the female administrator as imitating the aggressive male executive (for example, see Henning & Jardim, 1977). By contrast, Chernesky (1998) points to both subtle and blatant organizational-level explanations that impede or that are not conducive to opportunities in management for women. These can include "biases and stereotyping that discriminate against women, as well as organizational cultures and workplace environments that may be inhospitable to women" (p. 206). Chernesky suggests a set of managerial strategies that can advance women in the managerial ranks:

- identify gender inequities in the organization
- give women access to influence and power
- provide opportunities for women to showcase their managerial potential
- create new and alternative paths to the top that are not linked to gender
- dismantle the traditional hierarchical structure
- recognize that women bring to management a particular approach, orientation, or style that is valuable to organizations
- cultivate an organizational culture that does not tolerate discrimination or harassment and encourages raising concerns about gender discrimination
- establish organizational mechanisms specifically for the purpose of putting women on the fast track and shattering the glass ceiling. (1998, pp. 212–213)

Ethnic Minorities

Most social work organizations believe that having a diverse staff, including at administrative levels, is a positive goal, because the faces in the agency need to reflect those in its community and client base. However, problems persist in the ways that ethnic minorities are hired, evaluated, paid, and promoted within these organizations (Gummer, 1998).

As a result, obstacles and dilemmas persist for nonwhite social work administrators, as discussed in a unique article published decades ago (Vargus, 1980). Beginning with the hiring process, the external context creates a pressure as affirmative action programs engender reactions among nonminority colleagues that are frequently not expressed openly. Is the minority administrator hired for his or her competence or primarily as a gesture to the minority community or the funding agency? Once in the position, is the administrator over-identified with his or her own minority group? Does the minority administrator have to continuously be a superachiever to gain acceptance? Is the minority administrator expected to play a buffer or liaison role with the minority community over and above the normal expectations of the position? Do the minority group members expect the minority administrator to be a strong advocate on their behalf?

Brody (2000) provides guidelines for proactive leaders wishing to effectively develop and manage a diverse workforce. Many of these are directly aimed at fostering opportunities for ethnic minorities to access management positions within the agency. For example, measurable goals can be developed for promoting competent minorities. Progress for talented minorities can be encouraged by establishing teams or committees that offer opportunities to develop management skills. Management staff should be encouraged to examine their assumptions and expectations for minority staff persons and be sensitized to select and promote qualified individuals. Coaches, mentors, or personal advocates also can be assigned to minority staff members to encourage and support them in their goals for promotion.

Professional Context

Gummer (1979), in a trenchant analysis of the plight of social work administrators in the public sector, identifies them as an endangered species. This designation is apt not only for administrators in the public sector but also for social work administration in general. This leads to a focus on the problems created internally within a profession that is unprepared to face the fact that social work administrators operate on a different level and have different needs and priorities than their professional staff.

The following issues are highlighted because they are indicative of the dilemmas, tensions, constraints, and conflicts embedded in administrative practice in social work. Although these issues are posed as questions, they are directly related to administrative performance and to the elements identified earlier as being critical to the external context. These issues illustrate that both professional preparation and ongoing professional development are needed that are different from that which prepares social workers for direct practice.

Politics versus professionalism. Given the increased politicization of social service, can a social work administrator protect the integrity of his or her professional commitments and concerns? At the same time, what are the political skills that the executive must master to effectively negotiate the external environment?

Accountability. Although social work administrators have traditionally focused on accountability to their clients, new discussions of accountability introduce different debates in this area. Are public social service agencies accountable to the taxpayer as opposed to the client or consumer? Can both efficiency and effectiveness be maximized? How does one get the staff buy-in that is necessary for the process? How can and should the administrator balance competing expectations of various stakeholders? Given the complexity of this arena, what preparation does the executive need and how can external consultants be helpful?

Bureaucratization versus debureaucratization. What organizational design is appropriate for the diverse programs in social service? Given the importance of the organizational environment, what is the appropriate model for organizational decision making? How can administrators resist the temptation to mimic bureaucratic structures of other agencies or funders?

Technology. Given the continuous developments in administrative technologies, as discussed earlier, how does the social work administrator make the appropriate decisions in the use of the technologies and in the selection of consultants or technical experts? What are the dilemmas inherent in the introduction of unwanted or feared technologies to staff members?

The declining societal commitment to social work. Given that the commitment of the federal government to the support of human services is steadily eroding, and thus social work, in Gummer's terms (1979), may be an "endangered species," what is the responsibility of the social work administrator both inside and outside the organizational setting? How can the executive promote interprofessional collaboration where the unique contribution of the social worker is needed? How does the administrator balance competing organizational and professional demands for her or his attention?

The professional use of self. What are the essential interpersonal skills needed not only to maximize the effectiveness of the administrator's role but also to empower agency staff in their working environment? The interpersonal skills needed here are similar to those of the direct practitioner but additionally require a mix with organizational requirements. For example, knowing how to administer meetings (e.g., board and staff) requires a different set of interpersonal and organizational skills.

These issues are indeed critical ones, and social work administrators must be prepared to deal with them. The proactive leadership role of the social work administrator involves developing organizational systems that support and enhance professional issues for social workers. The advocacy role requires communication of organizational structures and processes that threaten professional integrity.

Labor Relations and Professionalism

The human service sector is undergoing dramatic change, with new organizational collaborations and mergers; downsizing; legal challenges; and union negotiations, arbitration, and mediation. Executives are facing serious challenges as they deal with the increasing complexity of labor relations. Becoming familiar with the legal issues involved is a necessity (Perlmutter, Bailey, & Netting, 2001).

At the same time, the growth of unions is taking hold among many professional groups, including social workers, in both the public and the voluntary sectors (Tambor, 1995). The negotiation process inherent in collective bargaining is the direct responsibility of the social work administrator.

The administrator often experiences personal conflicts regarding this process for several reasons. First, it is not surprising that conflict occurs because, frequently, the social work administrator has been a supporter of the trade union movement either on an abstract, ideological level or on a direct, personal level as a staff member of a professional local union. Being placed in the adversarial role of administrator can create great personal tensions as one crosses the picket line or even sits across the bargaining table as the representative of management. Second, social work administrators often view themselves as devoted to and involved with their staffs and are consequently unprepared for the feelings of rejection and betrayal they experience when their staff members decide to unionize.

In either case, it is essential that the administrator recognizes and deals with these feelings, as illustrated by the following case example.

Jack Forrest has always been an active union supporter, yet during a long-term strike he went to his office regularly, covered the telephones, and did what was necessary to keep the agency functioning at a minimal level. When asked by his young associate how he dealt with the conflict inherent in the situation, he responded that his role was that of administrator and that the different parties had their own roles to play. There was never any acrimony in his attitude as he met his staff members. This was in sharp contrast to another administrator who was angry, felt betrayed, and developed serious physical symptoms because he personalized the process.

The bottom line for the social work administrator is dealing fairly with the staff, being aware of the best pay and benefits packages in the geographic area, and playing an active role with the board of directors in interpreting and developing appropriate responses to their concerns. This is an unexplored area; there is a need for more serious attention to the administrative responsibility in collective bargaining, both in research and practice (Perlmutter et al., 2001).

A Final Word on the Context of Social Work Administration

Leadership in social work administration is critical for the success of social welfare programs in terms of both efficiency and effectiveness. The problems created for social work administration are complex and stem from external as well as internal forces.

In addition to the complexity described above, the administration of social programs in both the public and the private sectors is suddenly of interest to an array of new stakeholders. These stakeholders are primarily concerned with fiscal rather than client priorities. It is not surprising that, in the desperate effort to curtail costs, boards of directors of social service agencies have looked to business administrators to solve their agencies' fiscal problems. The problems remain complex, however, and resolution of these problems is not clear-cut.

What is clear is that social work administration requires a broad array of competencies in addition to ideological commitments and service delivery skills. The challenges are great for the social work profession to retain leadership in the field, and opportunities are numerous for creative and charismatic leadership. It is also clear, however, that administration is not for the faint of heart; rather, it is for those who are heartened by these provocative and demanding situations and who are ready to attain the competencies requisite to the task.

CHAPTER 3
Making the Shift from Practice to Administration

Two questions are frequently asked by social work practitioners: "Would I enjoy administration?" and "Would I be effective as a social work administrator?" These questions reflect several factors. First, knowledge about what the administrator actually does is often unclear. Second, the technical aspects of administration are unfamiliar and often threatening. Third, the practitioner is in conflict about abandoning the client caseload but is simultaneously driven by the hope that his or her leadership can make things work better in the agency. And finally, the practitioner may have conflicting feelings about anticipated changes in relationships with former peers. These conflicts are unfortunately exacerbated by the occasional negative perceptions of administration and administrators who are viewed in an adversarial role.

This chapter seeks to address these questions by discussing two topics of major importance. The first focuses on the personal perspective that is essential in making the shift from practice to administration. The second discusses the often unclear roles of the social work administrator and how they build on and differ from the role of the practitioner.

The Personal Perspective

In chapter 1 we stated that opportunities for promotions within agencies may arise that lead practitioners to consider making the shift to social work administration. The practitioner, in these situations, may be reacting to suggestions made by others or may be simply responding to internal job postings. In contrast, in other situations practitioners may proactively make decisions to market themselves as they seek to be considered for upcoming opportunities for advancement.

In either case practitioners must consider the skills and attributes they bring to the administrative role or those they must develop in order to be taken seriously. They must also take into account potential hurdles, both internal and external, to their successful transition to administration. In a sense, social workers considering making the shift must both advocate for themselves and manage their own changes. Finally, the issue concerning the use of power and authority comes into play throughout.

(1) Advocating for Yourself

Social workers initially may consider the phrase "advocating for yourself" to be in conflict with their perceptions of the traditional role of social workers: to advocate for others. However, whether the social worker is proactively working toward a career in administration or reacting to an opportunity for advancement that presents itself, she or he must be able to communicate her or his readiness for the administrative role. This implies persuasion, whereby the social worker encourages the individual(s) responsible for the promotional decision to consider him or her for the job; this is a form of advocacy.

One place to start is to assess the skills of the successful practitioner in terms of those needed in the administrative arena. A relevant question is the following: What skills have I developed as a practitioner that will help me be a successful administrator? Practitioners use many management skills in their roles as direct service workers; however, they are not typically thought of in this way. Some examples include the following:

- When social workers squeeze several home visits or counseling sessions into a busy workweek, they are performing time management.
- When social workers develop new referral sources for their clients, they are developing external resources.
- When social workers suggest changes to agency forms to make them more efficient, they are planning.
- When social workers convince their colleagues to form a case conferencing committee, they are organizing.
- When social workers work with colleagues in other agencies to form advocacy groups, they are networking.
- When social workers identify ways to better meet clients' needs within the agency, they are problem solving.

Recognizing this strong basis for administrative practice is an important beginning in the transition. Thus, the social work practitioner who wants to advocate for him or herself for an administrative position within the agency will begin this process by communicating the various ways he or she successfully used administrative skills while he or she was a practitioner.

In addition, the social worker who is ready to move into the administrative arena should also seek to attend management workshops or seminars. Often the agency will sponsor this attendance, as it provides supervisors with the information of the practitioner's interest in advancement within the organization, an important piece of information designed to promote a stable workforce in the agency. The following exemplifies this process:

Jane was an executive director who routinely used a "Career Ladder" as part of the annual performance review process. This practice helped her to know when staff members were feeling ready to proceed to administrative positions and helped them clarify their career goals. It was especially important for the executive to know how to cultivate good workers so they would stay with the agency.

One year, as Jane, the agency director, was evaluating the performance of a direct-care worker, she was surprised to discover that Sharon was interested in moving into management in the future. Because Sharon was an extremely valued employee, Jane was motivated to assist her in reaching her goals within the agency. At the same time, Jane did not want to lose her as a direct-care worker who was respected by her coworkers and clients alike, a real dilemma!

In discussing several options, they came up with the following plan: Sharon would have an administrative experience, as she would take responsibility for developing and managing a telephone information and referral service for the clients, both current and potential. Her salary was increased to reflect these additional responsibilities, and Jane provided in-service training as she guided her in the development of this new program. Sharon was extremely successful, and the service grew into an integral part of the organization. This was truly a win-win situation: Sharon's job was more interesting to her than before; she developed new management skills; the agency and its clients benefited from the service; and Jane kept the services of her wonderful direct-care worker for a few more years!

(2) Managing Your Own Change

Troubling questions often plague the practitioner who is considering the shift to administration: What will happen to my peer relationships? How can I be a successful administrator without abusing my power? Can I be an effective leader? This section will provide some insights into these questions.

It is inevitable that peer relationships will change when one is making the transition from direct practice to administration. Some of these will be positive and others will be perceived as negative. Positive outcomes from advancement into administration include increased respect from former peers, increased self-esteem from successfully adapting to management, and the development of new peer relationships with other managers and administrators. Negative outcomes must also be expected:

Mike was a practitioner in an agency serving people with mental retardation. Both he and his good friend and practitioner colleague, Curt, applied for the same administrative job within the agency. They discussed this situation before and during the time that they were both considered for the job and they agreed that whatever happened, they would remain friends and respectful colleagues.

When Mike got the job the relationship both inside and outside of the agency began to fall apart. Curt was very resentful of Mike's success, found it very hard to be managed by him, and resisted his authority. Mike had to decide which was more important: to try to salvage whatever was left of the relationship or to serve the agency's clients effectively in his new management role. He decided on the latter and hoped that the bonds they had developed as friends would eventually overcome the negative feelings provoked by this change.

This example shows that a very difficult part of making the decision to move from practitioner to administrator is the potential for negative changes in peer relationships.

It is extremely difficult to move up the ladder in one's own agency. It is essential that the administrator recognize that there needs to be a change in his or her professional relationships and must seek other contacts. External networks provide an opportunity to brainstorm about administrative situations with other administrators outside of the agency. It also may be the case, in the management of your own change, that if you are ready to move into administration, this goal can best be accomplished by shifting to another agency.

(3) The Use of Power and Authority

A major issue on a personal level is the effective use of power and authority, which is implicit in the administrative role and is often a source of tension. Social workers typically believe that power relationships have no place in their work; moreover, power is thought of as a negative. However, a large part of the job of social work administrators involves the use of authority in bureaucratic organizations, which inevitably implies power.

Gummer (1990) states that "even though the use of power may be alien to political and professional ideologies, social workers *do* exercise power in their work" (p. 119). The reality is that social workers control access to resources that their clients need; similarly, managers control access to resources that their staff members need. Just as the effective social worker uses this power to ensure that clients get the resources they need, the effective manager works to ensure that supervisees get the resources they need to do their jobs effectively. For these reasons, social workers considering the shift to administration can reject negative definitions of power and the fear that accompanies these definitions in favor of a determination to wield authority in positive ways that benefit clients, workers, and the entire agency.

To summarize, the personal perspective involves advocating for yourself, managing your own change, and effectively using power and authority. The effect of shifting from practitioner to administrator may be positive or negative on the family; both possibilities must be considered. Positive effects may involve regular working hours (for example, a daytime schedule instead of shift work), increased income, and elimination of on-call responsibilities. Negative effects on the family may include stress from increased responsibilities and longer workdays. With open communication and inclusive planning, the negative effects can be minimized.

What is critical is that the practitioner be aware of the many new aspects that will come into play on a personal level. Because knowledge is power, this knowledge should increase your confidence when applying for an administrative position within your agency or elsewhere.

The Systems Perspective

A systems perspective must also accompany the personal perspective, as a change in lenses is necessary in making the transition from direct practice to administration. This entails shifting from a focus on the unique and particular aspects of one's caseload to a broader perspective that focuses on the agency as a whole. Consequently, it is essential to understand the full effect of the shift so that the process of changing hats can be least disruptive. Although the direct practitioner must have a systems perspective, the critical distinction is in the focus of the work and the span of the activity, as illustrated in Table 1-1.

A systems perspective entails several new vantage points. The administrator must relate to members of other professions and disciplines within and outside the agency. This entails sensitivity to different languages, techniques, and value frameworks. Furthermore, administrators must work with public agencies, local governments, foundations, community groups, news media, and a host of other systems that have contact with the agency. In this arena, the higher the level of operation, the broader the scope of contacts.

A mapping of the agency as a system is effectively presented in Slavin's concept of "the organizational life space" of a social service agency (1980, p. 11). Slavin identifies the three basic elements of the social agency as a social system: the provider of the service (that is, practitioner), the user of the service (that is, client, consumer), and the organization (that is, the social agency). Each of these elements is embedded in a network that includes both internal and external constituencies, all of which are of concern to the administrator. The applicability of these concepts is illustrated through a case example following Figure 3-1.

FIGURE 3-1
Organizational Life Space of Social Administration:
Constituencies of Social Administrators

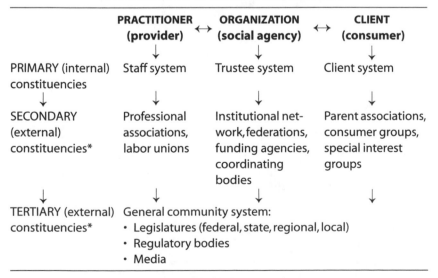

	PRACTITIONER (provider) ↔	ORGANIZATION (social agency) ↔	CLIENT (consumer)
	↓	↓	↓
PRIMARY (internal) constituencies	Staff system	Trustee system	Client system
↓	↓	↓	↓
SECONDARY (external) constituencies*	Professional associations, labor unions	Institutional network, federations, funding agencies, coordinating bodies	Parent associations, consumer groups, special interest groups
↓	↓	↓	↓
TERTIARY (external) constituencies*	General community system: • Legislatures (federal, state, regional, local) • Regulatory bodies • Media		

*These are illustrative and are not intended to be comprehensive

Case Example of Organizational Life Space: A Shelter for Battered Women

Agency Background

Womanspace, Inc., is a program that provides services to victims of domestic violence and sexual assault with a mission dedicated to improving the lives of women and their families. Currently celebrating 25 years of service to its community, the agency was established in response to the community's identified need for services addressing the social problem of domestic violence. More than 50 local organizations worked to develop plans for the agency, which opened its doors in 1978. The agency provides crisis intervention, systems advocacy, counseling and training, education, and technical assistance to the community. Since its inception, Womanspace has assisted over 30,000 women and 4,500 children who have experienced the tragedy of domestic violence, provided training for more than 30,000 professionals, and responded to nearly 107,000 crisis telephone calls (Womanspace, 2002).

The agency has developed multiple programs to meet the needs of its consumers. In addition to its emergency shelter, it offers a long-term transitional housing program, residential services for developmentally disabled women, counseling and support services, empowerment workshops, a legal clinic, a training and education program, a Chaplaincy Program, and sexual assault support services.

Womanspace as a Social System

To understand the agency as a whole, with a systems view, the administrator must attend both to the contextual variables, as discussed in Chapter 2, and to the variables within the organizational life space, as formulated by Slavin (1980).

In brief, the contextual environment of Womanspace is exceedingly turbulent, with constant change and shifts in all of the dimensions to be considered. Society's values and attitudes regarding domestic violence are not only in flux but also are, at times, in conflict with those of the agency.

Great passion is expressed, and the agency works continuously to educate the community about the issues surrounding family violence.

Every aspect of the agency's work is politicized, ranging from initial advocacy for statewide and national coalitions for battered women as well as a state government division on women to ongoing efforts to influence local, state, and federal legislation for support of its programs and the needs of its clients. This demands sophisticated political behavior on the part of the administrator.

A critical factor that must be taken into consideration is whether the organization is free-standing and autonomous or whether it is part of a larger system, or a host setting, such as a social work department located in a hospital. The consequences have great significance in determining the administrator's degree of freedom. Because Womanspace is freestanding, the administrator and the board of directors are in total control of the service.

Consequently, the assumptions that underlie the concept of administrative behavior as formulated in Chapter 1 are applicable here. An effective social work administrator is client-oriented and proactive and empowers the client-consumer, board of directors, and staff cohorts to become politically active as well.

Womanspace's Life Space

Womanspace effectively illustrates Slavin's (1980) construct of organizational life space and its three critical elements: (1) the organization itself, (2) the provider of the service (the practitioner), and (3) the user (the client-consumer) of the service.

Concerning the organization itself, the primary internal constituency is the trustee system that includes the board of directors and its policy-making function. The founders of Womanspace made two critical decisions in this regard. First, the board was carefully composed of representatives from various external interests: the legal profession, service providers, private business, and community members. Second, it would be composed primarily of women, in support of the belief that the agency addressed feminist issues.

Secondary constituencies that are external to but directly involved with Womanspace play a vital role. Of great importance is the connection with a network of feminist organizations in other areas of the state and country with which the agency can discuss ideas and issues. The agency has also developed partnerships with the state university's women's center as well as with other community organizations working toward common goals. These networks have helped the agency stay in tune with the larger feminist movement as well as with emerging service trends.

Governmental as well as nongovernmental funders are also important secondary constituencies for Womanspace. United Way, state grants, membership fees, and proceeds from a state marriage license tax generate support for the agency's programs. Womanspace is accountable to each of these sources of funds for the provision of effective services.

According to Slavin's (1980) formulation, the administrator must also deal with the external tertiary constituencies.

External tertiary constituencies are powerful influences on Womanspace. State legislation is aimed at the prevention of domestic violence and requires, for example, training for individual law enforcement officers that may be provided by nonprofit organizations such as Womanspace. Thus, the agency must develop and maintain effective working relationships with law enforcement agencies to provide input into training curricula or the training itself. News media are another critical tertiary element with which continuous and active contact is required, especially because a large part of Womanspace's efforts are aimed at community education.

In regard to practitioners, the second element identified in Slavin's organizational life space, Womanspace presents a complicated picture because it employs a diverse group of workers. This primary constituency consists of nonprofessionals, volunteers, and social workers. Volunteers fulfill an especially important role by tutoring adults and children, working at community events, providing childcare, and providing direct supportive services at the time of crisis. Thus, Womanspace employs people with a broad array of both sociological and educational backgrounds. The administrator must be cognizant of the diverse values, orientations, skills, experiences, interests, and needs of these different groups.

A unique consideration for Womanspace concerning its staff is related to safety, because working in the area of domestic violence is dangerous. Although the location of the emergency shelter is not publicized, from time to time abusers learn its whereabouts and appear at the door. Staff members have also been followed by abusers and subjected to personal threats because they are perceived as keeping shelter residents from them. For these reasons the agency is dedicated to protecting the safety of all staff, volunteers, and residents and does not permit individual names to appear in any agency publications, press releases, or other public media.

The third element in Slavin's organizational life space model is consumers.

For Womanspace, the element of consumers also requires attention to safety; empowerment is also paramount. When new residents come to the emergency shelter, they are asked to provide a physical description of their abuser. This is then used to identify potential unwanted or dangerous visitors to the shelter. Empowerment is key, and early in its development Womanspace determined that its role was to keep women safe, whether they chose to leave their abusers or not. Specifically, women who decide to stay with or return to their abusers are provided with survival tips and are never derided for their life choice.

The involvement of battered women with elements from the general community system is very important to Womanspace. Those women who are in stable (that is, nonviolent) situations and choose to assist the agency in its efforts educate the community often participate in speaking and training engagements or meet with legislators. The agency knows that survivors of domestic violence can provide powerful messages of tragedy and triumph.

Understanding the Whole

The complexity of the social service agency as a social system is evident, because it includes internal and external elements and primary, secondary, and tertiary constituencies. It must be emphasized that one's position within the organization determines one's vantage point.

Thus, a consumer will view Womanspace from her service needs and experiences; a board member will be mission oriented and concerned with the development and use of resources to meet organizational goals; staff members will focus on their specific work responsibilities, agency policies, and salary and benefits issues.

It is the agency administrator who must be aware of and responsive to all these aspects of the organization.

The Role of the Social Work Administrator

Menefee (2000), in an overview of various studies describing what managers do, offers a model based on his research. Menefee's model of social work management roles consists of eleven roles:

1. Communicator: written and verbal information are communicated to stakeholders inside and outside of the organization to exchange resources and keep staff informed
2. Boundary Spanner: networking and collaboration with external stakeholders to establish and maintain relationships and exchange resources
3. Futurist-Innovator: anticipating trends in the external and internal environment to inform planning and long-term survival of the organization
4. Organizer: adapting organizational structures and processes to ensure appropriate staffing and flow of resources
5. Resource Administrator: attracting resources to the agency and managing their use within the organization
6. Evaluator: assessing the changing needs of the target population and evaluating programs for ongoing effectiveness
7. Policy Practitioner: interpreting, communicating, and advocating for policies at various levels to ensure that client and agency needs are met
8. Advocator: representing the needs of the target population to legislators and government administrators

9. Supervisor: supporting, coordinating, educating, and evaluating the work of staff members
10. Facilitator: empowering staff through training and modeling collaborative practice
11. Team Builder-Leader: encouraging and developing multidisciplinary, interdisciplinary, or intradisciplinary teams.

Reviewing these roles can give the practitioner a crystal ball perspective on what to expect when the shift to administration is accomplished. It should be clear that many of these roles are performed at the practitioner level with both clients and coworkers, and therefore the skills are easily transferable. Attributes of the administrator also mirror those of the practitioner: self-awareness, self-regulation, motivation, empathy, and social skill (Brody, 2000). The distinction, then, between the practitioner and administrator becomes the emphasis and orientation of these roles and attributes. The administrator spends more time and uses a more comprehensive, external orientation than the practitioner.

Making the Shift

Dramatic changes are necessary in making the shift from direct practice to administration, and concerns about leadership abilities in relation to this broader systems focus come to the fore. Throughout the discussion the reader can assess her or his capacities and interests for leadership and return to Table 1-1 for a review of the primary activities of the three practice levels. Brody (2000) described traits and competencies that leaders must have to contribute to the effectiveness of their agencies. These are articulating a future orientation, being a social entrepreneur, treating staff with dignity, communicating significant messages, engendering trust, and inspiring top-level performance.

Leaders who articulate a future orientation work to improve the status quo, and they are "continuously working to help their organizations grow and change to meet new situations" (Brody, 2000, p. 12). Being a social entrepreneur means that the leader articulates a vision for the organization and implements activities in support of that vision. Leaders who treat staff with dignity consciously foster supportive environments in which they communicate empathy and compassion for their supervisees. Effective leaders communicate significant messages to their staff by making information clear, inviting input from supervisees, and relating tasks to the mission of the agency. Engendering trust requires that the leader fulfill promises, demonstrate consistency in decision making, and lead by example. Finally, leaders who inspire top-level performance establish achievable expectations and create opportunities for success. The following case example provides insight into these leadership roles.

Darnell was hired as the new director of a homeless shelter. There had been two interim directors over the last year, and the agency was floundering. One of the first things he did was to meet with his staff and board members to revisit the agency's mission. He wanted to be able to articulate a future orientation, so he hired a consultant to facilitate a planning session that included staff, volunteer clients, and board members to develop a vision statement for the agency. This was accomplished, and all constituents were in agreement regarding the direction the agency needed to take. A series of planning sessions were then held to develop strategies for implementing the mission.

Darnell identified a problem within the agency that reflected a lack of respect and trust among staff. He announced at a general staff meeting that he had an open-door policy and articulated his expectation that all staff would treat each other and clients respectfully, encouraging any individual who felt disrespected to meet with him. He learned that a component of the lack of trust was related to poor communications within the agency, so he instituted weekly staff meetings designed to ensure that important information about agency policies and procedures would be known to all.

It was equally important to Darnell that his staff members incorporate a success orientation. Therefore, he implemented a process whereby the annual performance evaluation served as the vehicle for agreeing on achievable and measurable work expectations so that opportunities for advancement and recognition could be developed.

This case provides us with a view of how administrators can thoughtfully demonstrate the traits and competencies necessary for the effectiveness of their agencies.

A Final Word on Making the Shift from Practice to Administration

This chapter has identified an array of different perspectives and behaviors implicit in administration from a personal vantage point. The following questions may help the reader to understand these perspectives and behaviors: Are they of interest to you? Do they intrigue you? Are you stimulated to think about the questions that have been raised and the issues that have been identified? Are you challenged to use your knowledge of direct practice and client needs in a different manner? Do you want to develop a totally different set of professional skills and approaches?

One student specializing in social work administration questioned whether he was suited for administration because he did not have an active style or charismatic personality. He was responding to a stereotype of the aggressive executive, but there are different needs for different leadership styles and approaches, and not every administrator is a charismatic leader. Much depends on the particular organizational requirements. The challenge is to understand the system and to be able to assess creatively the appropriate leadership approach for that setting at that point in the agency's development.

Some administrators excel in some areas; others excel in other areas. The trick is to "know thyself" and to assess the particular position to determine whether the position is appropriate in terms of individual interests, skills, and experiences. It also should be noted that administrators do not have to do everything themselves; they do some things themselves, whereas other assignments can be delegated to others. The bottom line is only that the task must be done effectively, because the administrator is responsible for the total operation.

There is no one route to travel for a meaningful career in social work. There are, indeed, different strokes for different folks. Every productive participant in the social service agency makes an important contribution. Perhaps the most important indicators are the individual's gut reactions to the ideas presented in this volume. The challenge then is to determine the level at which one wishes to work and then to broaden one's knowledge and skills to perform that job effectively. That said, the core values that social workers bring to both clinical and administrative practice are the same: service; social justice; dignity and worth of the person; importance of human relationships; integrity; and competence (NASW *Code of Ethics*, 1999). These values are critical at any level of social work practice.

The Dilemmas of
Middle Management

The route to administration usually begins with a promotion from frontline practice to middle management. Because the major thrust of this volume is to acquaint the reader with the administrative functions, this chapter focuses on the middle manager who is part of the administrative team. Table 1-1 contrasts the primary activities of the middle manager with those of direct care workers and administrators.

It has been noted that the major organizing principle for central administration is an external one, because administrators are affected by an array of requirements and pressures from sources in the environment, such as changing public policy, grant and contract requirements, and state and local politics. In dealing with these requirements, the focus is on "boundary spanning skills" (Edwards, Yankey, & Altpeter, 1998, p. 10).

In contrast to the external orientation of central administration, the major organizing principle of middle management is an internal one: the middle manager is the linchpin within the system who works totally on the inside and who deals with the effect of the external pressures on the agency. This internal role creates a situation in which the middle manager has no place to hide or escape. The organizational change function of middle managers is consequently circumscribed and complex, creating a middle management bind. Thus, middle managers have multiple foci for their advocacy role: frontline workers, entire programs, and even central administration.

There are three major types of constraints experienced by middle management within the agency system. Each of these constraints is discussed below, and the discussions are illustrated and clarified through the use of case material. Specific strategies are suggested that will aid middle managers not only in exhibiting effective individual performance but also in creating a more effective organizational structure.

The Environmental Context

Before discussing middle management, it is necessary to examine the context within which the middle management bind exists. This bind embodies the culmination of several decades of radical shifts in the nation's attitudes and policies in social welfare as well as the internal practice orientations of the social work profession.

The profession has always struggled with conflicting interests and issues: the conflict between settlement workers and charity organization workers; the role of social action and advocacy (Lee, 1937); whether social workers should work only in private agencies as opposed to public ones; and whether social workers should be unionized (Aronson, 1985; Tambor, 1995).

Traditional casework was the primary approach used in social work agencies. Since it was the one that was developed at the initial stage of the emergence of social work as a profession, and since it was the approach taught in the graduate programs of schools of social work, it was the one that was most clearly articulated and utilized. At the same time it was the most respected. Consequently social workers in other specializations were often envious of the position of social casework and felt the need for a comparable theoretical and methodological articulation for their specialities.

However the 1960s brought many changes to the profession. The emerging concern with populations at risk, as opposed to individuals in need, served to challenge the existing primacy of social casework practice. Furthermore, it was articulated that the effectiveness of the casework method even for individual clients had not been demon-strated. Consequently new voices were being heard.

This criticism of the profession was supported by many leading scholars who questioned the profession's indifference to research find-ings and methods. The quest for service effectiveness became an over-riding theme of this period, supported by new research findings (Meyer, Borgatta, & Jones, 1965).

The 1960s thus were years of upheaval as the problem that con-fronted social work during that period was that the change was never in any consistent direction; it was more like an uncontrolled ping-pong game than a climb up Mount Everest (Austin, 2000; Brager & Holloway, 1978).

Two new federal programs had a strong impact on the profession: the Community Mental Health Centers and the War on Poverty. And the new publicly funded programs stimulated a new debate concern-ing the form and function of organizational administrative apparatus in this radically revised context (Marris & Rein, 1968).

Furthermore, the civil rights movement and the antipoverty pro-gram raised challenging questions regarding the profession. Identifi-cation of the social worker with the social service agency, a bureaucratic stance, was viewed as incompatible with the primary requirement of meeting client needs. And there were additional challenges: the new use of manpower, new personnel, a community orientation, and com-munity participation.

It was clear that traditional social service agencies involved with family counseling, child guidance, and mental health would have to undergo a sharp self examination as a result of the aforementioned concerns. And new approaches would have to be explored in order to meet the challenges of the changing times.

Professionals in middle management positions were directly affected by these external challenges that required internal responses. Gummer captures the dilemmas facing social work managers in this era:

Discussions of multiple goals within social service organizations began in earnest in the 1960s with the appearance of a number of studies in which the authors argued that the stated goal of services for clients was only one of several goals. Other, un-stated goals included the maintenance and enhancement of the agency; isolation and control of people deemed deviant or dis-ruptive to the social order; defusion of resentment against the established social, economic, and political system; diversion of the dispossessed from taking political action; and provision of career opportunities for the growing number of human service professionals. (1990, p. 8)

In the 1970s a different spirit prevailed as social work was con-fronted by the age of accountability. Questions of service effective-ness gave way to concerns about the fundamental efficacy of human service organizations to respond to service groups they claim to serve, to use service techniques consistently, to demonstrate their effective-ness, and to manage public and private resources efficiently (Hawkins & Gunther, 1998). Middle managers were confronted with a host of new demands, requirements, pressures, and resistances as the actual nitty-gritty of accountability implementation was thrust at them, which was a far cry indeed from the pressures of the 1960s.

While attempting to grapple with both effectiveness and efficiency in their jobs, middle managers, along with central administration, were swept away by yet another shift, analogous more to a tidal wave than to a ping-pong game or a mountain climb. This shift was the wave of the 1980s with its mammoth cuts, reductions in force, and phase outs, which middle managers had to implement and deal with either at the front line or very close to it. In this neoconservative environment managers were faced with new imperatives for financial entrepreneurship, involvement with the process of contract manage-ment, and shifting patterns of funding (Austin, 2000).

In the 1990s new environmental pressures on human service man-agers emerged. Trends, such as managed care funding for social ser-vices, merging of nonprofit organizations, even greater demands for accountability, and privatization, have brought with them increased expectations for managerial responses. Hawkins and Gunther (1998) describe the challenge this way:

Managers in the 21st century, faced with the rapid change of social policy mandates and the challenge of creating effective, efficient, and quality-based delivery systems, are being called on to create organizational systems that are flexible and responsive to their environmental contexts and at the same time are expected to sustain administrative control in the goals, structure, and internal processes of their organizations. (p. 550)

Middle managers are certainly affected, given that "the *raison d'être* of the social administrator is client well-being and that the principle task of the manager is to facilitate that well-being" (Rapp & Poertner, 1992, p. 16). The challenge remains enabling this important professional group to be effective in its attempts to facilitate client well-being, function within human service agencies, and simultaneously meet personal needs for positive self-evaluation.

Constraints on Middle Management

A discussion of constraints on middle management facilitates an understanding of the pressures and problems ex–perienced by these professionals and can serve as a critical first step in developing a strategy for effective performance. Three types of constraints on middle management—professional, organizational, and personal—are discussed here. Although there is overlap between and among these three constraints, for heuristic purposes each constraint is identified and discussed and then is illustrated with case material from a public, county-based child welfare agency that offers services to dependent, neglected, or court-referred children and youths.

Professional Constraints

This discussion focuses on three variables that are often associated with professionals in social work: values, skill, and knowledge (Council on Social Work Education, 2002). Core values have been incorporated into the NASW *Code of Ethics* (1999) and include service, social justice, dignity and worth of the person, importance of human relationships, integrity, and competence. Social work managers face potential dilemmas when "values, and the professional duties that stem from them, conflict" (Reamer, 2000, p. 77).

Middle managers in social service agencies are placed in a bind when their social work values run counter to those of the community.

For example, a child welfare agency was placed at great risk when the broader community, which gave it both sanction and support, withdrew its commitment to the welfare of children in exchange for a commitment to a Proposition 13-type tax economy, which placed a cap on property taxes. The political result was to require that services be provided to children in their own homes as opposed to foster care, because this appeared to be the less costly route. In reality, the children would be short-changed, because the need for more supervision and more extensive supports would, in fact, be more costly. (It should be noted that this entire discussion took place in a different context than that of the current views concerning family preservation.)

Although the strategy for providing services to children in their own homes as opposed to placement ostensibly was trumpeted as the preferred route for the sake of the children, a position which rationalized the belief that services at home are cheaper than foster care, when push came to shove funding was the dominant force even when it was clearly detrimental to the children. Although the executive director of the agency was active in dealing with the external boundary system and advocating for children, it was the middle manager who had to make this practice operational, which was incompatible with social work values of the time, and confront frontline staff and clients directly.

The skill requirement within this discussion of professional constraints created a bind, because these middle managers were not prepared technically to do the work. Consequently, they were in a bind because the job expectations continuously expanded as the funding decreased. Although the agency closed one of its three branch offices as well as its emergency shelter, the needs in the community did not shrink proportionately; consequently, the remaining two branch offices picked up the extra load. The middle managers were running themselves ragged, as they continued to function as they had in the previous context, because they did not have the appropriate administrative tools at their disposal to conceptualize a different design for their work. Thus, for example, they continued to do individual supervision because this was the way it had always been done and this was the way they had been trained—except that now there were simply not enough hours in the day, or days in the week, to meet the numerous new demands made upon them.

The final variable within the discussion of professionalism relates to knowledge, in this case an understanding of the constantly changing public policies that guide the practice of both the public and private social service agencies. Given the turbulence of the current human service environment, administrators face the dual dilemma of processing and refining an enormous amount of information from the environment as well as developing appropriate mechanisms for the transmission of this information to the relevant staff members.

This discussion of professional constraints, as illustrated by the problems in values, skill, and knowledge, serves to highlight the important relationship between ideology and competence as the necessary ingredients for social change. The implications of this discussion for strategies for change are discussed below.

Organizational Constraints

An understanding of organizational constraints from a theoretical perspective should provide middle managers with a way of dealing with the structure and dynamics of their social service systems. Four types of organizational constraints are presented here: (1) the nature of the agency's purpose, (2) the organization as an unstable system, (3) the expectations of superordinates (that is, central administration), and (4) the expectations of subordinates.

The first, and major, organizational constraint is that of agency purpose, in that social agencies must deal with the most complex, intractable social problems in society, and the organization, by its very nature, bears a special burden. The challenges that arise from difficult social problems, such as homelessness or spousal abuse, often mean that middle managers are on call lest an emergency arises, and emergencies are certainly far from being the exception.

The second organizational constraint is that of an unstable system, meaning that it is impossible to work with the assurance and support of a steady, ongoing working structure. Carefully and systematically developed plans, procedures, and practices can be obsolete within an exceedingly short time. The problem was identified above as it affected the middle managers' technical competence; here the focus is on the organizational dilemmas created by the frequent cuts and reorganizations, such as staff cuts and the resulting restructuring of jobs or downsizing of agencies.

The third organizational constraint results from the expectations placed on middle managers by central administration. The pressures experienced by central administration often cause it to impose unrealistic expectations and demands on middle management in response to its own administrative bind. Too often a weak relationship exists between the two groups, leading to little communication as well as a great deal of frustration and hostility. Each group views the other as insensitive, unresponsive, and even incompetent. There is little opportunity for each group to view the situation from the other's perspective. Consequently, the bind becomes more constricting on both groups.

Finally, there is the organizational constraint created by expectations from subordinates. Gummer (1990) observes "there is evidence . . . that social agency supervisors and workers are increasingly experiencing goal conflicts" (p. 75). These conflicts can arise from increasing scarcity of resources, perceived by frontline workers as the managers' reorientation from service needs to those related to fiscal concerns. Tropman's (1998) discussion of effective group decision making focuses on creative management of competing values and interests throughout the organization. It is clear that middle managers who desire positive outcomes for clients must attend to the satisfaction of their supervisees. There is no question that organizational constraints exacerbate the bind experienced by middle managers.

Personal Constraints

Although the constraints discussed in this section are frequently addressed within an organizational or professional framework, the intent here is to emphasize that the costs are indeed personal and that there is much personal *sturm und drang* in the process. Although the strategies that follow are organizationally based and organizationally oriented, the discussion is framed around three personal constraints: feelings of inadequacy; racial, gender, and other diversity concerns; and burnout.

The move from frontline practitioner to middle manager creates identity problems for any clinician, whether that direct practitioner is a social worker, educator, or psychiatrist. Lewis, Lewis, Packard, and Souflée (2001) identify multiple transitional issues for the direct practitioner moving to the supervisory role. These issues include

- shifting perceptions of clients, from individual to program or agency perspectives
- movement from encouraging clients to motivating workers
- change from colleague to evaluator of workers
- responsibility for policy formulation rather than implementation
- exercise of authority and responsibility for workers' failures
- relinquishing satisfying direct relationships with clients.

Those very qualities that are supported and encouraged in the development of a clinician are often antithetical to executive performance. The greatest problem area is in the use of power and authority. Whereas the direct practitioner is trained in the avoidance of coercive authority, middle managers must develop a sense of purpose and responsibility for ensuring that decisions are carried out.

The middle managers in the child welfare agency previously discussed experienced these tensions. They felt extremely uncomfortable both in making demands and in imposing sanctions, and they felt extremely inadequate in their capacity to stimulate the staff members to ensure that high-quality work was being performed.

The various types of diversity, particularly those associated with racial and gender concerns, also create personal tensions. Although there has been an increase in diversity of the workforce that is likely to continue, Menefee (2000) deplores the lack of information on the roles of minority managers: "There has been no research published relating ethnicity to what managers do and why they do it" (p. 258). According to the 1995 survey of NASW members, a considerable portion of ethnic minorities reported administration and management as their primary function: 20.8 percent of African Americans; 20.6 percent of Puerto Ricans; 18.3 percent of Asian Americans; 15.6 percent of Native Americans; 13.8 percent of Chicanos; and 13 percent of other Hispanics (Gibelman & Schervish, 1997). Pressures of tokenism, differential assignments, and institutionalized attitudes of racism persist as challenges to minority managers (Gummer, 1990) also apply to women, gay, and lesbian professionals. Preferences for the straight, white, nonethnic male are still in evidence. It is clear that there is a continuing need for attention to diversity (Gallos, Ramsey, & Associates, 1997).

Burnout, the third personal constraint, is related to the increasing pressures of the job both in terms of the complexity of the problems faced by the clients and the larger workload. The problem is accentuated by poor communication with central administration, as discussed earlier. Central administration was viewed by middle management as being totally externally oriented, inconsistent in expectations, peremptory in demands, not understanding of complex work problems, nonsupportive of staff to the external constituencies, and indifferent to high-quality performance. Koeske and Koeske (2000) tell us "by far the most studied worker variables in the literature on human service workers have been burnout and attitude toward the job (that is, job satisfaction)" (p. 226). Workers may perceive inequity when they believe they are unappreciated or the organization is unresponsive to their needs; this, in turn, can lead to burnout. Furthermore, although empirical evidence has not yet supported theories relating expectations to burnout, there is widespread belief that workers who hold unrealistic expectations for their clients might experience burnout because of perceptions of unreciprocated efforts (Koeske & Koeske, 2000).

The effects of these various stressors on middle management are to create anxiety, depression, and self-deprecation, and it is important to recognize that "supervisors . . . can burn out, and they need feedback, support, and interaction in their own work lives" (Lewis et al., 2001, p. 146). Personal constraints are complex and are induced by an array of difficult external realities. Clearly, they extract a toll from the individuals who are at risk in these middle management positions, for they are truly caught in between.

Strategies for Change: The Task of Empowerment

Empowerment means both to give formal authority to and to enable. The assumption underpinning this discussion is that in their administrative roles, middle managers are empowered to work for improvement and change within their organizations. This focus on empowerment is based on Maslow's (1976) assumption that humans like to participate in their own fate, and that given sufficient information they will make wise decisions about their own lives—that they prefer to have a say in everything that affects their future.

Thus, an empowered middle manager would be particularly sensitive to the continuous internal and external shifts affecting clients, services, and the agency. The empowered middle manager would assume an initiating role in relation to these various events to fine-tune the services on a continuing basis to meet client needs. The empowered middle manager would provide an environment that would stimulate professionals at all levels in the organization to take more responsibility for their own performance, growth, and development. Finally, the empowered middle manager would use his or her position to advocate with central administration for necessary change.

Empowerment is based on three assumptions. First, it is essential to understand the situation at a conceptual level as a first step to deal with it. Second, although conceptual clarity is necessary, it is insufficient and must be accompanied by technical clarity (that is, the nitty-gritty of how to do it). Third, the strategies to be developed must be appropriate and compatible with the individual's position in the organization.

This discussion of strategies is organized and derived from the professional, organizational, and personal constraints identified previously. The strategies are designed to deal with three levels within the organization. Middle managers must learn how to work effectively with their own peer group (that is, other middle managers). Middle managers must learn how to take the initiative in defining their needs with central administration. Finally, middle managers must learn how to work effectively with line staff (that is, their supervisees). It is important to realize that these strategies can be successful only if they are developed within a context of overall organizational empowerment involving all levels of the organization (that is, top management, middle management, line workers, and clients).

Professional Strategies

Values, skills, and knowledge were identified earlier as professional constraints on middle management. An empowered middle manager has the capacity to manage change in the following ways. In regard to values, the ideological tensions experienced by middle managers are never unique to them but affect workers at all levels of the agency. Middle management is certainly in the position to initiate and organize educational programs (for example, values clarification sessions) for themselves, their supervisees, and central administration. Thus, they can have an effect on the total agency system in a critical way as they identify and clarify the tensions and problems created by the conflict in values.

In the skills area, middle management can request on-the-job training or continuing education to update and improve their technical performance. In a turbulent environment, such as that of social work, it is impossible to keep abreast of technical changes, and it is essential that prior educational experiences be complemented and supplemented. For example, very specific skills in organizing a meeting, setting limits, and redefining expectations for staff performance can make an enormous difference with regard to empowerment and confidence in striving for change.

In addressing knowledge, middle management can request regularly scheduled informational sessions with central administration in which they are kept informed about changes in the external boundary systems.

Organizational Strategies

The four organizational constraints identified previously relate to the agency's purpose, the agency's instability, the expectations of superordinates (that is, central administration), and the expectations of subordinates (that is, supervisees). The strategies that are developed must take these constraints into account.

There is no question that social workers work in organizations that are designed to deal with the most complex and intractable social problems. This is a reality that affects the total agency system. Related to the constraint of the agency's precarious purpose are the constraints created by an unstable system.

A strategy that is appropriate and that empowers middle management is one that, again, addresses all levels of the agency, because the middle manager is in a central position to bring to the surface the problems created not only by the agency's precarious purpose but also by the shifting scene. It can be helpful for all levels of staff to understand that the problems faced by staff are based on reality and are not caused by personal inadequacy. The simple process of providing understanding and insight to staff members of the effects of these constraints can be a meaningful contribution not only to the system's effective functioning but also toward stimulating efforts to make the necessary changes to more effectively meet the agency's goals.

Regarding the expectations of superordinates, the process of empowerment enables middle managers to be more effective in dealing with central administration. If communications are poor and the perceptions are negative, middle managers should take the initiative and define new and effective methods of working with central administration.

For example, communications can be increased through both formal and informal mechanisms. Middle management can request a regular monthly meeting with central administration with formal agenda items related to policies, procedures, and other administrative business while simultaneously seeking to improve the relationship. This can be achieved, for example, by inviting the administrator to lunch without having a specific agenda. Middle management can initiate a suggestion box mechanism to help central administration be more informed of frontline realities and thus meet a need of central administration. Finally, middle management can request that central administration approve the development of a seminar series with outside speakers from, for example, other agencies or universities who can serve as a source of external stimulation to staff members who have few external contacts.

Regarding the expectations of supervisees, it is again possible to focus on organizational processes to improve this relationship. For example, it can be helpful for all branch offices in the organization to have similar middle management activities. There can be joint group supervision of workers who do the same type of work at all branch offices (for example, adoption or foster care). There can be training for employees throughout the agency, for those at the front line as well as for middle management, to help them to develop their leadership potential and to encourage them to initiate activities, such as planning educational meetings for specific areas of learning.

The possibilities are endless and are limited only by the particular staff in the particular setting. It can be a satisfying and stimulating process to empower middle managers to take hold of their positions and enable them to take the initiative and become experimental in their organizational efforts. This approach assumes not only that the middle manager but also the organization must take some risks, because the middle manager cannot do this alone. The hope is that it will stimulate continuous assessment and reassessment in the organization in regard to responsible growth and change as it seeks to provide high-quality service.

Personal Strategies

The personal constraints of feelings of inadequacy, racial or gender concerns, and burnout were discussed previously. The strategies that follow are designed to deal with these constraints and thus loosen the middle management bind. It is important to emphasize that this final set of strategies has been labeled "personal" for discussion purposes only. This does not mean simply a defect or problem on an individual level. The strategies must be viewed from a systems framework and must be directly related to the aforementioned professional and organizational constraints and strategies, given that the shift from clinician to manager is a difficult transition. It is essential that use of peer group structures, which have been suggested for dealing with the other constraints, be viewed as a primary strategy for dealing with these feelings of inadequacy. The peer group of middle managers can serve a self-help, mutual aid function by providing the opportunity for insight, clarification, and education. The support and trust that emerge can provide an important base for this group and can allow more task-oriented strategies to be worked out. When the group of middle managers in the child welfare agency recognized that their feelings of inadequacy were common to all members of the group, tremendous pressures were released, allowing them the freedom to explore other issues.

A different approach is required for dealing with diversity. An appropriate strategy is similar to that identified earlier in the discussion of precarious values. The entire agency must be the target for this intervention and requires an array of approaches appropriate to the particular situation. Perlmutter and associates (2001) present an action model for supporting diversity which has several phases, including identifying the need for change in the agency, "relating the concept of diversity to the organization's mission, vision and culture," providing education and training to staff to help them change, and continuously monitoring the process to assure a climate that supports diversity (p. 116).

Burnout must be carefully examined because it affects middle managers in the specific agency setting. Again, all levels in the agency hierarchy of employees must be considered, because employees at each level affect and impinge upon those at the other levels. For example, middle managers too often think that central administration views them as inadequate; consequently, it is essential that central administration provides the necessary supports and "stroking" as a first step. By making explicit their burnout reactions within their peer group, middle managers can begin to develop coping techniques together. Finally, middle managers must be sensitive to and deal with the needs of their supervisees. By developing action strategies to deal with this problem, feelings of burnout will be dealt with and reduced.

All the strategies in this discussion are examples of the changes an empowered manager is capable of making to have a more satisfied workforce and a more effective agency.

A Final Word on the Dilemmas of Middle Management

Brody (2000) effectively captured the zeitgeist of the middle manager by describing this role as "the pickle in the middle," referring to a children's game where a runner tries not to be captured between two bases.

> Managers are frequently the pickle in the middle, caught between the conflicting expectations of their bosses and those who work under their supervision. They are often called on to reconcile the expectations and policies of the organization with the concerns and needs of their subordinates . . . managerial loyalties can be pulled in several directions. Managers' abilities to connect the needs and requirements of one level of the organization to those of another ultimately determine their effectiveness. (pp. 191–192)

This chapter has identified a series of constraints faced by middle management and has presented an array of strategies to deal with these constraints within the conceptual framework of empowerment. This discussion, which takes social work values and applies them to the practice of administration, is important in a volume that deals with social work administration, because recognition of the needs of middle management is a major responsibility of central administration. It is not possible to deal with middle managers in isolation, because they are part of the agency as a social system.

CHAPTER 5

Administrative Advocacy and the Management of Change

The profession of social work is unique in its commitment to social change. This commitment is exemplified by the *Code of Ethics* of the NASW, which provides an important framework for the administrator's role in the initiation and implementation of change as it emphasizes the pursuit of justice and the shaping of social policies and institutions. This commitment applies to both middle and upper management.

The administrator in a human service agency is a key figure in administrative advocacy and the management of change. However, before we can discuss aspects of that role we must focus on the concept of institutional mission. The mission of an organization defines the organization and clarifies its purpose, its raison d'etre. The mission is shaped by the social problem the agency seeks to address and the values upon which the mission is based. In his classic work, Selznick (1957) calls attention to the centrality of mission and defines it as "the setting of goals . . . as a creative task. It entails a self assessment to discover the true commitments of the organization, as set by effective internal and external demands" (p. 62). Defining the agency's mission occurs, or should occur, at the initial organizational phase of formation and requires constant attention in response to the changing environment. This is a critical process in the life of the social service agency, because it is the intersection of values with governance and the framework for the setting of agency policy and programs. Administrative advocacy and the management of change consequently do not occur in a vacuum. They are shaped by the unique characteristics of the agency and its mission.

Levy (1979) focuses on the role of administrators in regard to advocacy and social change as he makes two central points. First, social administrators should support employees who seek to change agency practices or policies. Second, administrators throughout the organization should play a central role in creating a climate that supports the initiation and implementation of change. These lead to several underlying assumptions in this chapter.

A first assumption is that there must be a partnership among all levels of administration in a social agency in working for social change. Thus, middle managers must have the support of central administrators to be actors in the change process and vice versa. A second assumption of this discussion is that change is ongoing and continuous in every social agency, which must be responsive to an ever-changing social, economic, and political context as discussed in Chapter 2. The role of administrators is to be sensitive to the need for change and to manage the process to produce better outcomes for consumers of services. A third assumption is that a commitment to social change may be necessary, but it is certainly not sufficient. Careful analysis and strategic planning must precede the process if any change effort is to be successful.

This chapter examines the implications for administrators and explores the possibilities for organizational change both within the agency and in its external environment (Perlmutter & Gummer, 1995). A partnership among all agency administrators is essential, because the chief executive officers (CEOs) are usually the major actors in the external system and the middle managers are involved within and are in a position to have information concerning the effect of public policy on the consumers of service.

We begin the discussion with a working description of organizational change. We then discuss the dilemmas inherent in the change process and describe a model that can be helpful in organizing the change process. We conclude the chapter by suggesting some strategies for administrative action. Case material is used throughout to illustrate the various topics associated with organizational change. The intent of this discussion is to stimulate each administrator to determine an appropriate response that fits the specific people in the specific organization within its particular environment. This material is presented in Part 1 of this book, as it provides underpinnings and theoretical perspectives which apply to all aspects of administrative practice.

A Working Description of Organizational Change

There are many types of organizational change, ranging from small to large and from short-term to long-term, depending on the problem being addressed (Perlmutter & Gummer, 1995). Large-scale change is fundamental in nature and can transform the organization's "core form" (Haveman, 1992) and "distinctive character" (Selznick, 1957). Although it is often linked to external changes in the agency's policy or task environment, large-scale change can also be linked to internal stimuli. For example, the development of computer technology, an *external* scientific development, has certainly brought change to social agencies. Examples of *internal* stimuli are the unionization of agency staff or the decision to use BSWs in addition to MSWs to provide services to the clientele.

It is not unusual for an organization to change its status from being an informal self-help group, such as an AIDS support program, to becoming a formal social agency serving AIDS patients. This shift entails a basic change in the agency's grounds for legitimacy, and major administrative adjustments must be made in the shift from being an informal group with broad-based member involvement to becoming a formal bureaucratic structure. Similarly, when an organization shifts from a small nonprofit to a for-profit agency (for example, a preschool nursery is incorporated into a for-profit child care corporation), major changes occur not only in the policy arena but also in the professional one. Also, when an organization merges with another agency to survive and to protect its services (for example, two small mental health clinics become one entity), the consequences of this shift must be addressed. These are changes that begin at the upper administrative and board of directors levels but certainly involve all the administrative levels in the organizations.

Complementary to large-scale change is the importance of small change in organizational life, change that also challenges management at all levels. When a client group brings a new set of problems to the agency, a change in the professional repertoire may be needed: Mental health professionals working with individual clients may be faced with families requiring family interventions. When the agency, because of budget problems, closes its neighborhood-based services and centralization occurs, new caseloads and work arrangements are required. When new technology is introduced into the agency and the staff is extremely resistant, new staff development approaches are necessary.

Two examples illustrate the role of different levels of administration in dealing with change, both big and small. In the first, emphasis is on the awareness and involvement of all the staff members in the organization.

The mission of an AIDS Service Organization (ASO) was to promote quality of life by providing care for those with human immunodeficiency virus (HIV). This mission was called into question when the staff members throughout the organization recognized that the public's perception of HIV had shifted in recent years. They knew that although HIV/AIDS was formerly seen as a deadly disease, it was increasingly perceived to be a manageable illness because of new drug treatments. They believed that what sounded like good news for their clients could threaten their agency because it might draw attention and resources from the continuing grim facts about the HIV/AIDS epidemic. They feared that new funding would favor drug treatments over community-based services, such as education, prevention, and supportive services, to those already infected with HIV. Thus, they knew the environment was chaotic where (1) levels of new infections remained constant, (2) treatment and service needs of subpopulations were increasing, and (3) case management methodologies were shifting to adherence issues. However, policy and funding attention were diverted away from these critical issues in favor of medical interventions.

The ASO attempted to anticipate and prepare for changes in its external environment, and all staff members were involved in the process. Rather than face possible extinction because it was a community-based service organization, the members of the organization made a proactive decision to identify the possible effect of these environmental changes on the agency and plan for a survival response.

The second example illustrates how small change can be brought about within the social agency.

A social work student intern who was placed in a hospital social work department became aware of the long wait for service in the lab where clients went for medical tests. Her supervisor, the unit director, encouraged her to document her observations. The student went to observe the situation and found that the technicians were often oblivious to the problem, frequently chatted among themselves, and were not responsive to the patients in the waiting room. She observed the laboratory for a two-week period and systematically recorded the data. At the suggestion of the unit director she reported her findings at a social work staff meeting. The director of the social work unit exemplified the administrative role discussed in the introductory section of this chapter: She not only supported the student's effort, thus initiating the change process, but she also took the information to the appropriate channels to implement the change.

These examples illustrate the central role of administrators in initiating change, both big and small. In the first example the administrator recognized the importance of taking seriously staff members' observations regarding changes in the external environment. In the second example, the effectiveness of the middle manager was clear as she helped the student worker initiate the change and involved upper management in effecting the change.

Both examples demonstrate the importance of the organization's ability to be flexible and responsive to various elements in the system, including the consumers and the staff, as the organization continuously seeks to be more effective and more efficient. Both of these instances demonstrate that it is essential that administrators analyze and understand the potential consequences for the organization and the consumers of the service.

Dilemmas Inherent in Organizational Change

Because the processes of initiating and implementing organizational change are not simple or obvious, one should understand some of the possible dilemmas and constraints inherent in the situation, which can help develop a clearer understanding and analysis as the basis for action (Handy, 1994).

A first, and major, dilemma, one that is always present, is the reality of the status quo pressures in organizational life, pressures that create inertia in all systems. The known is always safer than the unknown; risk-taking carries potential benefits but also potential liabilities. Consequently, changes needed in the professional arena are usually viewed as a threat to practitioners' identity and competency and are rarely seen as opportunities to broaden their repertoire of professional competencies and to grow in professional stature. Similarly, technological changes, such as the use of the Internet, are usually resisted by social workers who are less comfortable in the technical arena and who often argue that the changes will interfere with the worker-client relationship.

There are various ways that receptivity to change can be manifested within an organization, as illustrated by the following matrix.

The active–receptive quadrant represents those staff members who openly welcome and encourage efforts to change the organization, their jobs, or both. Passive–receptive staff members will comply

TABLE 5–1
Matrix of Receptivity to Change

	RECEPTIVE	OBSTRUCTIVE
ACTIVE	Engagement	Sabotage
PASSIVE	Reluctant Compliance	Noncompliance

reluctantly with the change effort. Those who work from the active–obstructive perspective will attempt to thwart or undermine efforts toward change. Finally, those who characterize the passive-obstructive quadrant will ignore changes they find threatening. It is important for administrators to judge staff members' readiness for change before undertaking projects that may result in obstructive behaviors and either plan for early education about myths that may underpin these concerns or revise change plans. On the other hand, administrators who have successfully fostered positive change cultures in their organizations can recognize and encourage receptivity to specific change projects.

The ASO provides interesting illustrative case material, as resistance to change was evident on all levels.

The implications for pressure to maintain the status quo were great in the ASO. Current clients of the agency were extremely concerned that even the effort to undertake any major change being considered might draw attention away from their ongoing needs and that the ultimate change might result in reduced service provision for them. Board members were concerned that an agency to which they had pledged their support might change to a new type of organization that would not be providing services that were aligned with their sociopolitical viewpoints. Also, staff members were concerned about being left out of any reconfiguration of services and believed their jobs might be threatened by any major change that might occur.

A second dilemma, and a fundamental one, is the conflict in values often experienced by social workers whose professional values differ from those of the broader society. As the United States has become more conservative, many of the values that underpin the profession of social work are being threatened. Given that social work is a profession committed to working with the poor, the disenfranchised, the disabled, and the elderly and with fighting homophobia and other "isms," it is often at odds with the larger society, which is increasingly less willing to support social programs that serve these vulnerable populations.

Social work administrators can too easily become co-opted by and assume the values of the larger society that create these conflicts. For example, the social work administrator who refused to serve Medicaid-eligible clients in a quest for fiscal efficiency (see Chapter 2) chose to adopt the values of the organizational environment. He abdicated leadership when he should have helped his board of directors take some risks to continue to meet the needs of this client group as well as to ensure that the mission of the organization was being fulfilled. The ASO also faced value issues:

The conflict in values that had previously been subordinated to immediate needs rose to the surface. The polarized views of care versus prevention and community care versus medical interventions were debated publicly with potentially tangible outcomes for the agency and its client population. These conflicting values were expressed both inside and outside the ASO, with an added layer of concerns related to the public's perception that medical advances had ended the HIV/AIDS epidemic. The debate became even more heated when the ASO's stakeholders (clients, staff, administrators, and board members) expressed divergent opinions regarding the potential for the ASO to become co-opted by the value system adopted by the larger society. Specifically they wondered if the agency would change its mission to ensure its own survival at the expense of the welfare of its current, and some believed, only legitimate client population.

The third dilemma we identify here concerns the issue of *advocacy* and is directly related to the administrators' role in social change. Social workers as advocates have long been viewed as central to the profession (Ad Hoc Committee on Advocacy, 1969). However, maintaining the advocacy role within human service organizations is never simple (Ostrander, 1989). Because nonprofits are often dependent on external grants and contracts that support their programs, they think that they are in a compromised position if they become advocates. This certainly puts administrators into a bind who face the reality of never biting the hand that feeds you.

One provocative argument suggests that agencies providing services to clients not only should not, but cannot, be effective advocates, because of their dependency on external funding. Instead, the position is that the advocacy function should be lodged in advocacy organizations or professional associations that can freely identify the problems and bring the issues to the public. This is in contrast to the strong views of several authors who argue that advocacy must be part of the ongoing leadership role in all human service organizations, a long-held and clearly articulated position in the social work literature (Ezell, 2001; Gibelman & Kraft, 1996; Haynes & Mickelson, 2000; Schneider & Lester, 2001).

In the case of the ASO this ambivalence was evident:

The issue of advocacy was central to those in the agency who agreed that something needed to be done, that inaction was not an option. Yet, ironically, many of these same individuals felt the pressure of conflicting mandates for advocacy and service provision. They wondered how the ASO could advocate effectively for systemic changes both inside and outside the agency while maintaining its legitimacy as a service provider.

Unfortunately, in reality the many pressures for survival faced by human service organizations often put advocacy at the bottom of the list of roles played by their executives (Perlmutter & Adams, 1994). Thus, a dilemma exists for social work administrators, who must take a position in regard to advocacy that requires careful analysis and consideration of their particular agency's circumstance.

This discussion identifies some of the dilemmas faced by social work administrators as they seek to initiate and implement change within their agencies. The more clearly the dilemmas inherent in the problem situation are understood, the better the possibility of developing an effective approach for the management of change.

A Model for Implementing Change

Various theoretical models of change are provided in the literature (for example, Brager & Holloway, 1978; Kettner, Daley, & Nichols, 1985; Netting, Kettner, & McMurtry, 1998). The remainder of this discussion focuses on a recent model of change and we begin with a graphic depiction of this change process (see table 5-2) (Lewis & Crook, 2001).

The first stage, identifying the problem, involves carefully defining and specifying the impetus for change, and it requires agreement among core stakeholders that a problem exists. As presented earlier in this chapter, the staff members of the ASO were the initiators of the change effort, as they observed the changing external environment and identified potential negative consequences for the agency. However, the recognition that core stakeholders also included the board of directors quickly made it evident to the executive director that the problem identification process had to include their input.

Based on information provided by staff members, the executive director decided to investigate the potential for board support of a change effort. The executive director met with a member of the board of directors who was knowledgeable about the trends in funding, technology, and value

TABLE 5–2
Organizational Change Model

Stage	Description
Identifying the problem	Agreement by initiator(s) that a problem exists
Initial information gathering	Verify the existence of the problem via input from funders or legitimizers
Forming a working group and agreeing on a change strategy	Include various staff members in defining a change strategy
Developing an action plan	Identify action steps, person(s) responsible, and products; establish a timeline
Implementing the action plan	Gather data, prepare reports
Gaining support from critical actors in the agency	Present data and proposal for change to key volunteers (board members) and clients
Approving and legitimizing the organizational change	Provide board members with sufficient data to approve required changes (for example mission statement, agency name)

systems. This individual confirmed her understanding of the problem and agreed to actively participate in planning activities alongside the staff of the agency.

Second, initial information gathering is important for verifying the existence and nature of the problem.

The data-gathering process included (1) a literature search to examine the background of the problem and precedents set by other organizations facing the same dilemma and (2) a survey of community informants. Staff members led this process, which involved consultation with the county health department and other key sources of information.

This is followed by the development of a working group. It is important to ensure that knowledgeable individuals have early buy-in for the change effort. In addition, ideas and perspectives can be shared in the group setting. Finally, the benefit of distributed effort cannot be understated in large-scale change, for it is impossible for one individual to successfully undertake major organizational change. The specific task facing the working group is to reach agreement on a change strategy and to develop an action plan for accomplishing the desired change.

The executive director formed a working group consisting of key staff members. The first task facing the working group was to agree on a change strategy. The group developed an action plan that would guide its efforts in gathering and presenting information necessary for the successful adoption of the change effort. The change strategy essentially consisted of gathering data, preparing a formal proposal, and garnering formal board of directors' approval for the change effort.

With information about the problem and the needs and capacities of the local community service system, the working group determined that the potential existed for expanding the agency's mission to include those with sexually transmitted diseases. An analysis of driving and restraining forces helped them assess the feasibility of the planned change effort.

The next two stages of the change model call for implementation of the action plan and gaining support from critical actors in the agency. Reports are prepared based on data gathered, further data that may be needed is identified, and involvement of all those who may be affected by the proposed change is ensured.

Two remaining concerns were support of all agency staff and potential funding for a revised agency orientation. First, the executive director met with the remaining agency staff members to determine their levels of support for the effort and to understand their concerns. Second, the director of fundraising was asked to identify potential sources of revenue for which the agency would be eligible to apply with an expanded service profile. Once support from all staff was secured and future funding sources were identified, the working group prepared a concise document with all identified information.

The executive director next met informally with the members of the board's executive committee and the client representative of the board of directors to discuss the proposal and request support at the formal board meeting. Many of the board members, as with many ASOs, had personal investments in the mission of the organization because of their own or their family's involvement with HIV/AIDS. Because of this, it was imperative that a primary purpose of the proposed change effort be made clear: to maintain current service levels to HIV-positive individuals and their families as well as provide additional services of which this population may be in need. These informal meetings were successful in garnering support from these key actors.

The final stage in the model involves approving and legitimizing the organizational change. In cases of large-scale change, this may require formal procedures involving the board of directors.

With the planning process complete, the key strategy for the agency was to change the agency's mission statement, which, because it was in the agency's bylaws, required following the procedure for revisions to that document. Following proper notice, a special meeting of the board was held to discuss the recommended changes to the agency's mission. The goal for the special meeting was to review the information in the informational document, hear from interested community stakeholders, and, pending adoption of the proposed changes, discuss changes to the mission statement.

Because the preparation had been so comprehensive for that meeting, the board of directors voted unanimously to proceed with the proposed change. With this vote, the agency expanded its service mission from serving people with HIV/AIDS to include people with other sexually transmitted diseases, hepatitis, and tuberculosis. The change effort was successful and the executive director and her staff proceeded to implement the new mission.

Although not included in the published model, a final stage that is critical would be evaluation and feedback. Both are essential to complete the change process, as they identify the success of the implementation of change and begin the next steps in a never-ending cycle.

What is of importance to us is that Lewis and Crook's (2001) model assumes that extensive participation of the various stakeholders throughout the process is essential. The receptiveness to new ideas and to innovation is directly related to the comfort level of the staff members. Therefore, the organizational climate should be examined to see how acknowledged, supported, and encouraged the staff members are. Are staff members merely given lip service or is it in fact a hospitable setting? Designing a change strategy certainly is an opportunity for broad involvement.

The Politics of Managing Change

Political strategies are usually viewed as applying to the broader political system in the agency environment as it affects the organization; these are usually seen as the major responsibility of the agency executive (Gardner, 1990; Perlmutter, 1980). However, political strategies are not important only externally but are equally important in the internal system (Perlmutter, 1983). Furthermore, they play an important role in providing data necessary to support the external political positions taken by the agency.

As early as 1980, Gummer focused on the power-politics model as critical in viewing the internal organization as a political arena.

The power-politics approach stems from the assumption of the ubiquity of self-interest as the motivating force in all human behavior, including behavior in organizations. Individuals in organizations will act to secure and promote their interests, these being determined by one's location in the structure. Action directed toward the interests of the organization as a whole . . . will occur only if there is some force operating to constrain self-interest behavior. (p. 46)

This perspective is important for administrative understanding as it makes explicit the self-interests of the actors within the organization and links them with the organizational interests of the total agency.

The reluctance of social work professionals to view power as part of their repertoire of skills is a long-standing problem and, indeed, a constraint. However, it is not unique to our profession. Pfeffer, concerned with all professions, persuasively argues that "unless and until we are willing to come to terms with organizational power and influence, and admit that the skills of getting things done are as important as the skills of figuring out what to do, our organizations will fall further and further behind" (1992, p. 32). Power is an implicit part of the professional agenda, both internally and externally.

The use of power and politics can be enhanced if all staff members are helped to broaden their vision and understanding both of their role and the broader political context that affects their agency. Methods for empowering staff should be explored and can include, for example, creating the possibility for administrators at all levels to be responsible for initiating policy discussions, suggesting agency priorities and agendas, and leading staff training and development sessions. Shera and Page (1995) present a trenchant discussion of this subject.

Patti and Resnick (1985) focus on the type of leadership needed to be effective in a broad array of agency settings. Their thoughts are most instructive, as they emphasize the need for flexibility in the leadership style to be used, an approach which is political in its implementation:

... leadership which falls on one end of the continuum as *directive* and that at the other end as *delegative*. The middle of the continuum we will call *participative* leadership. . . . The manager who uses a type of leadership at one point in the change process need not use that same style in successive steps. . . . While leadership may vary in each stage, it is probably true that it is easier to move from directive to more employee-centered styles, than vice versa. (pp. 275–276)

The bottom line for the effective initiation and implementation of change is that careful planning is required before implementation is attempted. The more information that is available to inform the process, the more familiarity with different models and methods of operation, the greater the chance for success. In the case of the ASO, the effective use of political strategies contributed to the success of the change effort. These included widespread and ongoing communication among all stakeholders, extensive planning, and documentation supporting recommendations. A commitment to expansion rather than replacement of the agency's purposes as well as its services all facilitated the final decision process.

A Final Word on Administrative Advocacy and the Management of Change

This chapter has presented some material designed to help social work administrators in their analysis and planning for the initiation and implementation of change. The discussion of the context of change, the types of change, the dilemmas inherent in change, and the model for action all form the basis for the development of intelligent strategies and approaches to the problem. The case example provides a real-world look at the application of these strategies. It also reflects the assumptions discussed at the beginning of the chapter: the importance of partnerships throughout the agency, the continuous nature of agency change, and the importance of careful analysis and strategic planning.

The process of change is complex, and there are no clear-cut right or wrong answers. Administrators must be ready to take risks, try new things, work with new networks, and adjust or even abandon earlier approaches. The bottom line is that social work administrators must be flexible, ready to consider new ideas and new approaches to their work. They must also recognize that "if you know your organization's strategy but your colleagues do not, you will have difficulty accomplishing anything" (Pfeffer, 1992, p. 36).

PART II

*ADMINISTRATIVE
PRACTICE
PERSPECTIVES*

CHAPTER 6

The Administrator's Role in Agency Governance

In the search for an understanding of the functions of the administrator of a social service agency, it is essential to focus on the governance process. Eadie (1999) observes the following:

> The pre-eminent leadership team of a nonprofit consists of its chief executive and its governing board, and the success of a nonprofit's . . . efforts depends heavily on how well the respective leadership roles are played and on how effectively the two parties work together. (p. 33)

This chapter discusses governance and the implications for administrative leadership, as boards determine agency policy but must work closely with the executive who provides stewardship for its implementation (Brody, 2000; Kettner, 2002). This discussion logically follows the preceding chapter, as governance and policy making are inextricably intertwined with the agency's mission.

The Structure of Governance

In the human services, organizational governance is related to the legal status of the organization (that is, its auspice):

[This] differentiates between the private [for-profit] provision of a service and the provision of that service by an organization set up by the community at large, either through government or voluntary association, with accountability for, and control over, the service resting with the community at large. Such control and accountability are in contrast to the private control of the contractual relationship mutually exercised by a private practitioner and his client. (Lowenstein, 1964, p. 4, cited in Gibelman, 2000, p. 114)

The governance function is located in the board of directors in the case of nonprofit organizations; in for-profit agencies, it may be one person or a group of people who own the company (Gibelman, 2000). In either case, the authority for governing the agency is specified in articles of incorporation, constitutions, or bylaws. These set forth operating procedures and mechanisms for naming or changing directors.

Citizen or consumer participation presents important opportunities and alternatives in the structure of governance. In the 1960s, for the first time the participation of consumers in affecting the policies of the agencies from which they received services was given credence over the traditional participation of the social elites who were not consumers of the agency's services. This notion has become a fact of social service agency life, although it is imperfectly implemented.

Experimentation in different models of decision making began to take place in the human services, usually in small agencies in the voluntary sector. Although large public bureaucracies are less receptive to these changes, innovations have been taking place there as well. Weil (2000) describes a number of instances in which "leaders in system reform favor the option of the public sector working collaboratively with nonprofits to develop a comprehensive community-based system" (p. 500). She notes early reports of success in Iowa, Missouri, and Florida, with such strategies as neighborhood-based interagency teams, partnerships with law enforcement developed in nonauthoritarian structures, and community safety projects.

Creative approaches to governance are sometimes driven by public policy; in the following example, the federal government attempted to enforce community participation in housing development as it sought to encourage nonprofits to sponsor housing development. The U.S. Department of Housing and Urban Development's HOME program is regulated by federal law 24 CFR Part 92.2, which

> establishes requirements for the organizational structure of a CHDO [Community Housing Development Organization] to ensure that the governing body of the organization is controlled by the community it serves. These requirements are designed to ensure that the CHDO is capable of decisions and actions that address the community's needs without undue influence from external agendas. (U.S. Department of Housing and Urban Development, 2002, p. 1)

In accordance with this law, CHDOs may provide homebuyer, rental assistance, homeowner rehabilitation, or tenant-based rental assistance programs. However, to be certified as a CHDO, a nonprofit organization must confirm that at least one-third of its board is comprised of representatives of the low-income community it serves, and no more than one-third of its board may be representatives of the public sector.

These new governing structural arrangements reflect broad societal shifts. The administrator has the opportunity to become informed about the pros and cons, the costs and benefits, of new governance mechanisms and to provide leadership in the agency as it seeks to define its appropriate governance structure.

The Board of Directors

A review of the historical development of board leadership in the voluntary social welfare highlights its changing role over time (Austin, 2000). In the last half of the 19th century, boards of trustees provided leadership in divergent ways. In charity agencies, board members often made case-related decisions, and their volunteer "friendly visitors" were typically board members' wives. By contrast, board members in settlement houses typically served a fundraising function, and the individual in charge of the house was the primary leader.

As social work became more professional, the role of the board became more delimited. The activities of concerned citizens who organize welfare services for various groups in need, both in sectarian and nonsectarian settings, has remained constant over time and represents a delimited aspect of policy making. The boards of voluntary agencies were originally comprised of wealthy laypeople whose function was often to provide funds for the agency; however, with the advent of community-wide, federated fund raising (for example, United Way, Black United Fund), their functions changed and broadened. Today, the board

> carries out a range of vital functions for any non-profit organization. Its members—sometimes called "trustees," "overseers," or "directors"—are people in whom power is entrusted by the community to act as fiduciaries and to guide their organizations with caring, skill, and integrity. They represent the voice of society and are expected to act on behalf of the interests of the community, constituents, and sponsors. Creating, nurturing, and renewing this core group of leaders are basic requisites for an organization's survival and effectiveness. (Holland, 1999, p. 425)

In addition to policy making, other critical roles of the board of directors include strategic planning, fiscal oversight, and resource development, as well as nurturing relationships with the community. Furthermore, the board delegates specific roles to agency executives and managers and creates substructures to carry out the work of the agency.

Social welfare is big business today. Current estimates of combined government (federal, state, and local) spending on human service programs exceed $200 billion annually (Martin, 2000). Consequently, the fiduciary function of boards has increased in importance and board members now are often expected either to contribute or to raise specified amounts of money annually. This creates tensions for board members who are serving for reasons other than their wealth.

The diversity of the board also requires attention. Community representation is key for organizational effectiveness and can be achieved via board membership and other means:

Mechanisms for community input in the agency planning and decision-making process can be institutionalized through policy. Board diversity can be mandated by policy, and this diversity can boost organizational responsiveness by granting the community a voice in the agency. The community's voice can also be heard through the creation of special community advisory boards or task forces that are formalized in agency policy. The resources that community residents bring to the board, advisory group, or task force are perceived as just as valuable as the resources brought by affluent board members. (Iglehart, 2000, p. 441)

Today, the board–administrator relationship is recognized as essential for agency effectiveness. The board and the executive must work well together as they seek to assure that the agency is meeting its mission and is effectively serving its community (Brody, 2000). Each benefits from this mutuality—the executive director receives support for his or her professional objectives, including career advancement, and the board members provide community sanction while meeting their individual, professional, and social needs. Moreover, the effective board–staff partnership can contribute to a positive organizational culture (Gibelman, 2003).

The Role of the Administrator

The role of the administrator in relation to the board of directors is a complex one for several reasons. First, not only are administrators hired by the agency's board of directors, but the board also has the power to fire them. Second, the administrator is trained to protect professional social work values, knowledge, and skill, in contrast to the board members, whose expertise is usually in legal and fiscal matters. Finally, not unimportant is the fact that the board is usually composed of community elites, while the administrator is usually a member of the upwardly mobile middle class.

The role of the administrator in interaction with the board of directors is multifaceted. Although the conventional understanding is that the board is responsible for determining policies and that the administrator is responsible for implementing those policies, in reality the process is far from cut and dried. The administrator is most often critical in determining the nature and the extent of the relationship.

The most obvious and clear-cut roles of the administrator are in hiring staff to carry out board policies through program implementation and in developing and monitoring the budget. This is part of the full-time commitment of the administrator, in contrast with that of the board members, who are volunteers with primary responsibilities elsewhere. The administrator provides agency statistics, interprets present and future client needs, discusses service options, and provides information on funding possibilities. Since the board members are dependent in their decision making on the material supplied by the administrator, the administrator is very much part of the policy-making process.

The administrator can be proactive, reactive, content to rest on the agency's laurels, or innovative in responding to the rapidly changing needs of the community. The administrator of a family service agency, for example, can be content to support the stance that the agency should continue business as usual with the traditional families in the community. Alternatively, the administrator can seek to serve people who are part of the many new and unconventional family arrangements, including single heads of households, gay and lesbian partners with children, or families that have members with AIDS. There is no question that the latter choice would be a more complicated, costly, and controversial route. Also, it is important that the board be informed and involved in this shift, which is a service expansion within the administrator's domain but nevertheless can provoke unexpected board reactions. This is an opportunity for the administrator to educate and develop the board.

Another example of administrative choice is the decision concerning agency survival when the budget is not balanced. An administrator whose agency is experiencing financial hardship can opt to restrict service to paying clients and refer the poor population to a public agency. By contrast, the administrator who is a client advocate can ask the board to consider new approaches to fundraising or the use of a portion of the agency's endowment funds to assure the continuation of services for economically dependent clients.

A powerful tool that administrators have at their disposal is the ability to influence the composition of the board of directors to reflect the direction the administrator deems appropriate for future agency development. This process occurs in the context of joint decision making between leaders on the board of directors and the administrator. While the board is ultimately responsible for voting in new members, it is common for considerable planning and negotiating to take place before the new member is presented for consideration at a meeting. Typically, the administrator meets with the nominating committee to discuss potential candidates for a board position. Because administrators have contact with many different professionals in the community in the normal course of conducting business, they develop relationships that may prove beneficial to the board. It is critical to acknowledge that these relationships may, indeed, also prove beneficial for the administrator's political agenda.

Board members can be recommended for a variety of reasons, including their ideological orientation in relation to community and client needs, their financial capability, their political and social connections, their technical expertise, or a combination of these. An analysis of the external environment and an analysis of the agency's mission and priorities form the basis for these recommendations. A case example illustrates this point.

Manuel was hired as the new executive director for a small agency providing a variety of services to children. He had worked for many years in the community served by the agency and had developed exciting ideas that he hoped to implement in his new role.

However, he quickly learned that his board of directors, while dedicated and capable, lacked enthusiasm for what they considered to be risky undertakings. At various times in his first year, Manuel felt that his innovations were being blocked by his conservative board.

Manuel developed a strategy whereby he approached individuals whom he knew to be inspirational leaders to learn of their interest in board membership. He then arranged lunch meetings during which they could meet the agency's board president. In these meetings he carefully articulated what he believed to be common values and shared beliefs held by the potential board member and the sitting board of directors. He succeeded in gaining approval for these new members at the board's subsequent meetings.

This strategy paid off in the long term, because within two years, the board's composition had changed to one that was diverse as well as open to innovation. The new members brought resources and enthusiasm to the board and, partly because of their initial relationships with Manuel, tended to support his proposals.

This case demonstrates the use of the nomination process in agenda setting for the agency. It also illustrates the potential influence of proactive leadership on board–staff relationships and, ultimately, organizational effectiveness.

Policy Issues of Administrative Concern

It is helpful to understand some of the critical issues and dilemmas that are addressed in the governance process of social service agencies. This issue is at the heart of the policy and management process in social agencies because choices must be made and priorities set which are compatible with the mission of the agency.

An issue of central concern at the social policy level is that of privatization of the social services. In Chapter 2 we noted the shift from traditional nonprofit agencies to profit-making agencies in the social service sector as an element of a turbulent environment. Nonprofit social service agencies are also being pressured to consider alternative means of raising financial resources, because public funds have become less available for social service and community funds have not kept pace with society's needs. One new approach is for nonprofits to offer for-profit activities (for example, museum shops in art museums).

However, it is not at all clear that these for-profit activities do, in fact, yield a profit (Adams & Perlmutter, 1991; Ezell, 2000). So the question that boards must ask is whether they should venture into commercial activity or continue with the more traditional means of funding.

Other issues continuously surface. How should social work deal with the issue of effectiveness versus efficiency? In the early years of voluntary social service agency activity, effectiveness was the central criterion for service, and services were ipso facto accepted at face value. However, in the 1970s a new emphasis on accountability arose with public contracting for nonprofit social services.

This dual emphasis requires that boards of directors and agency administrators become active partners in identifying ways to improve both quality and efficiency. At the same time they must develop means for ensuring that resources are not diverted from service provision, which is related to effectiveness, to service monitoring, which is related to efficiency.

The final policy issue in this discussion, of importance in today's environment of shrinking financial resources, concerns the issue of agency autonomy.

The Jewish Employment and Vocational Service of Philadelphia is a major contractor with the Pennsylvania Department of Public Welfare in providing employment and training services to welfare recipients. The state is ready to give the agency more and more contracts for more and more services, both in expansion of existing programs and in developing new ones. While this is very tempting from a financial point of view, the agency faces the dilemma of becoming an arm of the Department of Public Welfare and not focusing on other communal issues, needs, programs, and resources. Some board members have raised an objection to further contracting with the state, and this is indeed a critical dilemma and a critical decision that the agency must make.

Gibelman (2000) highlights this concern in the following statement: "The consequences of contracting have been seen as so pervasive that nonprofits have been accused of becoming agents of the state" (p. 127). The tendency of nonprofit agencies to adopt bureaucratic structures as a reflection of extensive government contracting is of growing concern.

These policy issues, among others, are illustrative of matters that require consideration, analysis, and decision making from both board and administration. How they are handled is a clear reflection of leadership style: "In ideal circumstances, the board and chief executive work closely together in determining directions and policies" (Brody, 2000, p. 312).

A Case in Point

Returning to the case study presented in Chapter 5, we find that many of the elements of agency governance discussed here apply.

The ASO had identified a potential threat to its long-term survival because of the changing external environment. The change agents in this case were the executive director and a member of the board of directors, who shared knowledge and concern about the implications of impending funding, technology, and values systems changes. Recall that the existing mission of the agency was to serve people with HIV/AIDS; because the change effort involved a potential revision of this mission, the involvement of the board of directors was essential.

By meeting informally with members of the board's executive committee and its client representative, the administrator acknowledged their key role in reaching the goal of major policy changes. This strategy also supported the importance of citizen input, as the board represented community members with personal investments in issues related to HIV/AIDS.

The change process also involved adherence to policy requirements for considering revision of the agency's mission. In so doing the board held a special meeting to review the information distributed by the working group and to decide on a revised mission statement, which it ultimately unanimously approved.

Three years later we see the effect of leadership and volunteer changes on the agency. The former executive director and many board members had left, and the new executive director and volunteers observed that the feared reduction of funding for HIV/AIDS services had not materialized. Subsequently, the new board revised the mission statement again to refocus the agency on HIV/AIDS community services.

From the outset this case illustrates the importance of an effective partnership between staff and board volunteers. These critical changes affect and reflect all aspects of the agency and concern competing values, interests, and stakeholders. A cohesive and unified approach is essential (Holland, 1999).

It is the administrator's responsibility to implement policy decisions made by the board (Gibelman, 2003). In the case of the ASO the new executive director found that she was unable to implement the previously approved mission statement and advocated for its reconsideration by the board in light of changing external circumstances.

Clearly, these new patterns reflect broad societal shifts. The administrator either can continue to work in a traditional mode or can seek to become informed about the pros and cons and the costs and benefits of new governance mechanisms to provide leadership in the agency as it seeks to define its appropriate governance structure (Perlmutter & Kramer, 2001).

A Final Word on Agency Governance

Boards of directors carry the legal responsibility and sanction for the agencies that they govern. It is clear, however, that their roles are dramatically shaped by and dependent on the administrators of their agencies. It is equally clear that the role of boards of directors is inextricably linked to administrators' roles in advocacy and the effective management of change.

The aim of this discussion has been to acquaint the reader with some of the issues that administrators must deal with as part of their normal workload. It is fair to state that the work the administrator performs with the board of directors is one of the more critical aspects of the job and requires careful and creative leadership.

The Administrator as Politician

Most social workers think of themselves as working outside the realm of politics. Although more than 170 social workers currently hold offices in national, state, and local government, this represents less than .03 percent of the total number of people who have social work degrees (NASW, 2003). In fact, the very word "politics" conjures negative images of aggressive and controlling behaviors on the part of individuals who seek personal gain. These connotations are all antithetical to what is considered professional social work behavior. However, another view of politics provides us with insight into the unavoidable and potentially beneficial political role that social workers can play. Kate Millet observed the following: "Change is the essence politics is supposed to be the means to bring into being" (1974, p. 567). Seen in this way, the social worker as change agent uses the political arena to achieve change—change that is grounded in advocacy for clients, workers, and social welfare organizations. Indeed, although most social workers do not hold political office, many are actively involved in political advocacy activities through professional associations and universities.

This chapter will discuss political activity that takes place both outside the organization and inside. Initially, the internal role of the social work administrator as politician will be presented. The focus is on the ability of the administrator to achieve change within the organization in a manner that betrays neither the well-being of clients nor the standing of the administrator. The second part of the chapter presents a discussion of the boundary-spanning political context of administrative practice.

The Internal Political Context

In most organizations that provide professional services, such as medicine, engineering, or social work, the route to the executive suite is charted by one's movement up the professional rungs. The implicit assumption is that if one is good at laying on hands, that is, providing a technical service, one can be effective at helping others lay on hands, and the movement is up the hierarchy of an organization. However, clinical skills do not ipso facto translate into administrative skills, even for first-class professionals. This is not to say that the concern is with the Peter Principle, whereby less than competent people are moved up to get them out. The concern is with qualified, competent, and meritorious practitioners having the necessary administrative skills.

Chapter 3 discussed the positive use of power within organizations to benefit both workers and clients. Gummer (1990), an astute commentator on the politics of social work administration, addressed the various political processes inherent in social welfare organizations. He framed his discussion around the contention that "politics is concerned with deciding about the distribution of scarce resources" (1990, p. 17). Gummer described five organizational features that characterize the political framework in organizations: "scarce resources, conflicting goals, uncertain technologies, multiple centers of power, and irreverent attitudes toward authority" (1990, p. 17). These are discussed below.

Scarce resources: Administrators must manage competing claims on limited resources. These resources include staff, funding, space, and even administrative attention. In complex social work organizations, competition can occur frequently. Conflicts among workers over access to agency vehicles or even copy machines must be managed by supervisors and administrators, often by compromises or trade-offs.

Administrators who are committed to ensuring the viability of their program units compete with each other to gain the resources they believe are necessary to successfully maintain or improve program outcomes. This competition can, in turn, require political activity on the part of the administrator.

Conflicting goals: Gummer (1990) offers insight into the potential for conflicts by stating that all social work organizations have multiple goals. Because these multiple goals are often addressed by multiple organizational subunits (for example, programs), the social administrator must manage the disparate organizational priorities that result. He or she may very well adopt a political strategy to advocate for the dominance of the goals of her or his program over others within the organization. For example, the resources for staffing a family life education program versus those for counseling services will require that the executive make choices about which one will be given priority. One major casework agency in New York City opted to close down its clinical services to individual clients and only serve broader family and community groups.

Uncertain technologies: Gummer defined technologies as "more or less certain methods for solving problems" (1990, p. 20). These can include service strategies (for example, counseling, job training, and so forth) as well as management information systems. The political process is used by administrators to manage conflicts among those who advocate for specific technologies over others. For example, should social workers continue the traditional means of recording or should they use computer technology? This process takes place through discussion, debate, and persuasion.

Multiple power centers: Power is acquired through multiple means: knowledge and expertise, education and experience, personal characteristics (for example, charisma), or by virtue of functional authority, that is, individuals' positions within organizations (Weinbach, 1990). Because there are multiple ways of attaining power, there can be conflicting overlaps within organizations that must be managed. For example, staff members may report to an individual who has functional authority over their jobs but may be supervised in their service provision by another person who has the education and experience to guide them in this regard. In this case the political process is used to maximize effective performance to sort out the ascendancy of authority in various situations encountered by workers.

Changing attitudes toward authority: Gummer defined authority as "legitimized power" (1990, p. 23) and observed that workers increasingly refuse to acknowledge its effect on their jobs. Trends in bottom-up decision making, whistle blowing, and information sharing have affected workers' unquestioned loyalty to the company line. The political challenge for administrators is to encourage constructive questioning and individual responsibility for outcomes while maintaining policy, program, and organizational integrity.

Rapp and Poertner (1992) summarized the inevitability of political behavior for social work administrators: "Every manager is confronted with a host of constituencies, each of whom makes demands which are often unsupportive of or incompatible with or irrelevant to organizational goal attainment and client welfare" (p. 15). Clearly, political effectiveness is related to the social administrator's capacity to thoughtfully and sensitively manage competing interests. Similarly, change that results from political behavior must take into account interests of all stakeholders.

The External Political Context

The social work administrator must be effective both internally and externally. As the external environment is simultaneously becoming more complex, dense, and unpredictable, special attention must be paid to new skills and strategies appropriate for a new political reality. Our professional organization, NASW, has highlighted the importance of these roles in its preamble to the *Code of Ethics*: "Social workers promote social justice and social change with and on behalf of clients" (1999). Underpinning this mandate is the expectation that political advocacy is required to work toward social justice and social change. The next section of this chapter discusses the current political environment as the context for the discussion of the administrator's role.

We previously highlighted the administrative role of boundary spanner (Menefee, 2000). This continuing need to explore the administrator's role regarding power, politics, and external boundaries guides this discussion. The particular interest here is in the practical consequences for the practicing administrator, because professionalism and politics are not disparate or incongruent activities. Rather, the social work administrator is the link between professionalism and politics.

The effects of increasing conservatism, begun in the 1980s and continuing through the new millennium, reverberate throughout American society as social programs are curtailed, dismembered, and dropped. The philosophical underpinnings that shape the social work profession have been called into question. This is indeed a shift for many social workers who were reared in a society that supported federal leadership in social programs, programs that provided services to a variety of populations in need and that encouraged labor development in human service. It is important to highlight the changes in ideology and national commitment.

During the 1990s, the word advocacy became the buzzword in professional social work. . . . Over the course of the decade, many social workers recognized the need to advocate for and on behalf of clients. . . . . In the interim, millions of individuals and families were directly impacted by the residual effects of federal and state policy initiatives. Of particular importance, entitlement programs crucial to the survival of vulnerable, displaced, and at-risk populations were devolved to state governments via block grants. Although block grants were not new to the 1990s, their specific aim was to decentralize the federal government's role and authority within existing social welfare programs while simultaneously reducing the federal government's budget. (Schneider & Lester, 2001, pp. 51–52)

The immediate realities faced by the administrator in dealing with policy and politics reflect this new policy context.

Policy and Politics

Because the areas of policy and politics are so closely intertwined, it is essential for the social work administrator to be clear about their similarities and differences. Policy is defined as program intentions that reflect decisions made on the basis of principles with supporting rationales. Politics is viewed as the actions of interest groups who are trying to affect or are affected by policies. The administrator must be well versed in both policy and politics.

Four policy constraints can be identified: sophisticated managerial responses are required to deal with mandates that are competing, conflicting, ambiguous, or incompatible (Perlmutter, 1980). Each constraint stems from external sources but is inextricably linked to internal operations. In the following discussion, the Personal Responsibility and Work Opportunity Reconciliation Act of 1996 (PRWORA) (P. L. 104-193) will be used as an example of each constraint. Specifically, the Temporary Assistance for Needy Families (TANF) program will be highlighted.

Competing mandates result when several policies that underpin a program are appropriate both on their own terms and with each other. A problem arises when no clear priorities have been set and resources are inadequate to support both programs. In TANF, welfare recipients are required to participate in job training activities, job placement activities, or both. The administration of these programs is left to states, consistent with PRWORA's decentralized approach. However, NASW recently advocated for increased educational and training opportunities for recipients because "current law restricts the ability of TANF recipients to improve their skills, the ability of states to best match recipients to the economic opportunities in their states, and the ability of businesses to access a pool of skilled workers" (Coalition Letter, 2002, p. 1). In this instance, recipients cannot meet work requirements (one mandate) because of the inability of the states to meet funding requirements (another mandate).

In dealing with competing mandates the appropriate strategy may be to garner increased resources to be able to fulfill the competing mandates simultaneously. If increased resources cannot be obtained, political advocacy, ordering of priorities, and long-range planning are necessary to ensure that both mandates are met.

In the case of *conflicting mandates* the administrator usually must choose to support one mandate or the other, not both. For example, some states developed transportation initiatives whereby TANF recipients receive free or low-cost automobiles but found that owner-ship of the vehicles increased recipients' asset worth to the point of disqualifying them for further government assistance. In some cases, an innovative administrator can use his or her analytical skills to re-define the problem and find different alternatives based on a new perspective; however, political advocacy may be needed to eliminate disincentives to client success.

Ambiguous mandates, which occur when expectations are unclear, can be used as an opportunity for creative leadership. The risk-taking administrator can take advantage of the lack of clarity and press for unconventional options and new directions. A less imaginative ad-ministrator might press for clarification of the policies and thus lose an opportunity for innovation. Furthermore, in the press for greater clarity the administrator could precipitate a less satisfactory situa-tion, particularly if an ambiguous mandate is reformulated into a com-peting or conflicting one.

Incompatible mandates reflect the different expectations of fed-eral, state, and local governments and create another administrative bind. The structure of PRWORA provides a direct example of this effect. Medicaid is administered by the federal government, cash benefits are administered by states, the Food Stamp program is ad-ministered by counties, and child care services are administered by local agencies. Many service providers as well as consumers did not understand that PRWORA decoupled Food Stamps (local) and Med-icaid (federal) from welfare benefits (state). As a result, many benefi-ciaries who could have benefited from food or health care services were left without these resources. This patchwork approach to ser-vice provision can be confusing to recipients and frustrating for social work administrators attempting to meet their clients' and agen-cies' needs.

Because public policy drives not only public but also voluntary agencies to an increasing degree, the expectations from each level of government are often diverse, and access to each level requires differ-ent skills (discussed in greater detail in the next section of this chap-ter). Policy is clearly bound to politics, and the administrator must become adept at differentiating the political skills needed to work effectively not only with bureaucracies at different levels but also with the broad array of interest groups at several levels.

Administrative Strategies

There is currently much discussion in the professional literature concerning administrative strategies for survival. Here the focus is on three approaches for proactive leadership linked to the preceding discussion of policies and politics: (1) working with the state system, (2) redesigning the voluntary sector, and (3) pursuing legal options. Each of these strategies is directed toward the external boundaries of the human service system.

Working with the State System

The role of government in social welfare has received a great deal of attention, and Schneider and Lester discuss the effect of the new federalism and the devolution of social welfare to the states:

> Power and authority are being transferred back to the states. It is important to note that these programs are crucial to the survival of vulnerable, displaced, and at-risk populations. Within broad federal guidelines, states have the flexibility to design, structure, and implement entitlement programs around their specific constituents or economies. (2001, p. 323)

As a politician, the social work administrator must be aware of the political ideology that informs the behavior of governors and legislators at the state level, where pragmatism overrides ideology. Thus, vested interests, limited resources, variations in interpreting legislative intent, public pressures, and opposition from oversight agencies are some of the pragmatic reasons why "deviation from legislative intent at the point of program initiation" may occur (Haynes & Michelson, 2000, p. 134).

An understanding of this reality is essential for the administrator to begin to develop effective approaches, and social work administrators are uniquely qualified for this task, which requires strong interaction skills. Haynes and Michelson (2000) suggest specific approaches, which include goal setting, strategy setting, lobbying, letter writing, and testifying.

Dissection of the anatomy of the state system provides clues to access. First, the governor's office, the executive branch, must be understood as an important point of entry, including the realities of gubernatorial succession and the statutory limitations on terms of office. This also means that the administrator should get to know members of the governor's immediate staff and their relationships to the established state agencies and their heads. An understanding of the budget office, which is within the executive branch, is critical, because there is an inherent relationship and tension between program and budget staffs.

Second, it is essential to examine the links among the three branches of government as well as to have access to key legislators and committees. Third, although commissioners are political appointees, management in the bureaucracy is ongoing; it is important to develop links at both the upper and middle management levels. Finally, the organization and mobilization of constituencies are essential and include consumers, providers, advocates, and professional associations. Constituencies link political, professional, and consumer interests. Not only are the political skills important, but the basic skill of community organizing also is a sine qua non.

Redesigning the Voluntary Sector

The voluntary sector, the traditional backbone of social work programs, is being revitalized in response to the shift in and diminution of public responsibility. It is time to reexamine the structure of this system, because it was originally designed and developed in a very different historical context.

The following strategies are illustrative selections. Social work administrators must help their voluntary agencies engage in strategic planning as they examine their raison d'etre, including the system variables of mission, services, and target populations. Business as usual, or organizational maintenance, cannot be continued when the external environment is shifting so dramatically. The planning must encompass not only the internal capacity but also the external capacity in the broader community as well.

This external orientation requires a new examination of the private sector, which now includes for-profit organizations that offer a broad array of human services. Can we relate to them? The capacity of emerging faith-based organizations to deliver effective service must also be reexamined. How do we relate to them (for example, by offering technical assistance, by mentoring, or what)?

Consequently, administrators, as well as their agencies, must become politically sophisticated and must sharpen their skills in dealing with the external environment. Administrators, for example, are in a unique position to know the consequences of the deregulation of many social programs. Although advocacy has always been viewed as a vital part of the social work profession's armamentarium, it must now be fine-tuned, expanded, and developed.

This reinforces the notion of the administrator as both politician and change agent. The relationship between these two roles is very clear and is essential in dealing with the many changes in the policy and service environments and in meeting clients' needs.

Pursuing Legal Options

The final external political strategy concerns the pursuit of legal remedies. This is an area that is usually unfamiliar to social work administrators, who often view it as being beyond their ken.

Ezell (2001) discusses a study of litigation activities undertaken by child advocacy organizations:

> Litigation was underutilized as an advocacy tool, but . . . litigation and advocacy to revise state statutes were the most successful of all activities. . . . It may be that advocates steer clear of confrontational tactics, preferring more collaborative or less costly approaches. Clearly, if advocates do not understand the potential of litigation, are not experienced or confident identifying circumstances when it is relevant, or they do not know how

to mobilize legal and other advocacy supports, this powerful advocacy tool might not be used. Sadly, the clients who are being ignored, underserved, or mistreated may have a longer wait for relief. (pp. 109–110)

Thus, social workers must consider legal options when developing advocacy strategies. The advantages of this route must be carefully weighed against the risks. Advantages include the right of complainants to be heard, accessibility, ascendance of principled arguments over costs, publicity for major successes, and the possibility of moving an intractable legislature to action on behalf of vulnerable populations. The risks, equally important to consider, primarily involve costs in terms of both time and money.

An example of legal advocacy efforts by social workers and service organizations can be found in The Arc of Colorado's (The Arc) efforts to reduce the waiting lists for services and programs. In 2000, The Arc supported the filing of a lawsuit, in the U.S. District Court in Colorado, by three individuals with developmental disabilities (the plaintiffs). These individuals were advocating for themselves as well as for 2,848 other persons with disabilities waiting for services. Waiting lists in the state ranged from 1 to 11 years.

The plaintiffs maintained that the State of Colorado violated its requirements under federal Medicaid laws for timely processing of service applications as well as provision of services, freedom of choice regarding services, and due process. They requested services in community-based settings that were home-like or waiver services based upon the choice of each person with a developmental disability seeking services. Based on the court-upheld principle of least restrictive environment, The Arc advocated for the prompt provision of small homes for those persons on the state's waiting list. Specifically, it sought the provision of funding by the State of Colorado to ensure the development and implementation of a consumer-directed service system.

Consistent with its mission of supporting and advocating for better quality of life for people with developmental disabilities, The Arc provided specific technical assistance to the plaintiffs in the form of recommended provisions for the settlement of the case, fact finding, and community education. A position statement was issued by The Arc in 2002. The Arc and other advocacy organizations have supported this lawsuit for over two years, at considerable cost in time and money. This is a long-term commitment, and by March 2002 the court had ruled only on pending motions related to the case. In response, The Arc filed a complaint the following month against the State of Colorado with the Office of Civil Rights.

This case example demonstrates the importance of legal advocacy in ensuring the rights of vulnerable populations. The admonishment to all social workers committed to social justice is evident: We must gain the skills needed for effective political activity in many different spheres, including legal environments.

A Final Word on Administration and Politics

This chapter focused on the role of the administrator as politician. It identified several areas for action, both internal and external to the social service agency, and presented a case illustration of the political activity on the part of social work administrators.

The social work administrator clearly is involved in politics in all aspects of the social service agency. The creative and sensitive use of the political process therefore becomes a central challenge and represents opportunities for proactive change management.

CHAPTER 8

The Administrator's Use of Communication

The interest in life does not lie in what people do, nor even in their relations to each other, but largely in the power to communicate with a third party, antagonistic, enigmatic, yet perhaps persuadable, which one may call life in general.

—Virginia Woolf, 1925

Communication is the glue that binds people together within an organization, given that "an organization is a group of people intentionally organized to accomplish an overall, common goal or set of goals" (McNamara, 1999, p. 1). Without effective communication, how is collective action toward common goals possible?

It is important to highlight the role of administrators at all levels in communication. Administrators communicate with staff internally and with other stakeholders externally as they seek to make clear agency services, agency needs, and program outcomes; set up evaluation systems for both employees and programs; and communicate relevant information to board members, funders, and other interested actors.

In this chapter we discuss the various ways that administrators make use of communication to build an effective agency. We focus on the differences in communication between administration and direct practice. Throughout the chapter we present illustrations from the field.

Two Basic Assumptions

(1) An Assumption of Advocacy

Throughout this volume we wish to emphasize the importance of the administrative role in advocacy and the management of change. The art of effective communication is critical in this endeavor, as the message is enhanced by the medium, which takes place in several ways. Advocacy is most effective when several stakeholders are involved. Helping staff understand their role in the advocacy process is critical, because the front line is where the needs are most evident. Communicating this information and developing a strategy with partners involves effective communication and makes collaborative efforts possible. Also, an awareness of the best methods of communication to use with the target audience (such as city councils, legislators, and foundations) is of equal importance. A case example of collective action that required extensive communication among stakeholders is provided below.

A social worker serving homeless individuals and families observed a disturbing trend in his caseload. It was apparent that his clients were not able to access government benefits for which they were eligible and which had the potential for contributing to their goals of self-sufficiency. These benefits included temporary welfare payments and food stamps, emergency rental assistance, and disability benefits.

He communicated with other service providers in his city and learned that similar observations had been made at their agencies. He organized a meeting of concerned providers, and the group rapidly identified the source of their frustration: The inaccessible benefit programs required a home address for eligibility, which was obviously not available to homeless people.

The group then cooperatively developed a strategy for addressing this problem. They agreed that their agencies were willing to serve as home base for their clients if the state legislature was willing to recognize service agency addresses for temporary use of homeless people when they applied for social welfare benefits. Their next step was to develop a plan for identifying a legislator who would sponsor a bill legitimizing the use of service agency addresses by homeless people applying for benefits.

The social worker who had initiated the community-wide response contacted a cooperative legislator. The bill was introduced and ultimately passed by the state legislature and was signed into law. Homeless people throughout the state could now use the addresses of shelters, lunch programs, and other agencies as temporary addresses, and a major barrier to ending their homelessness was removed.

This case example highlights the positive outcomes that may accrue from collective action and effective communication. This occurred throughout the service system but started with one social worker who recognized the need for advocacy as a means of supporting his efforts to serve his clients effectively. Communication, then, was the vehicle for systemic change. He initiated communication with other service providers as well as with policymakers, with the end result being an unprecedented change in a law that cost nothing and benefited many.

(2) Use of Technology

Professionals are increasingly called upon to utilize technology for communication purposes, whether it is in the form of sending and receiving electronic mail, presenting the agency through a Web page, or entering data regarding caseload characteristics and outcomes. In addition, they must obtain computer systems (including both hardware and software) that are responsive to the needs of all stakeholders, including workers, central administrators, board members, and funders. Administrators must also become involved in the development and management of computerized management information systems involving all aspects of the agency, including service provision and financial management.

It is of urgent importance that administrators recognize the pros and cons of technical modalities and use them selectively, and it is essential that the administrator work with the technological consultants to assure that the products being designed are client-oriented and user-friendly. All too often the technology serves as an impediment to clients, staff, or both.

For example, an automated telephone in a human service organization is often a source of great frustration for clients and discourages their potential use of the organization's services.

A large mental hospital had an automated phone system that required great skill in following the complex and intricate directions. You were told to push buttons, then told to push more buttons, then put on hold, and then often disconnected. The anxiety of patients who needed help was increased, and the hospital was viewed not as a helping resource but as another hindrance to getting help. This problem was called to the attention of administration, and great efforts were made to make the system more user-friendly.

In conclusion, the use of technology requires careful attention from a human perspective; it is not merely a technical problem.

Administrative Roles and the Use of Communication

Menefee's (2000) discussion of social work management roles (see Chapter 3) serves as a useful basis for our discussion of communication. It is important to examine how the effective use of communication enhances executive performance of many of these roles.

Communication with Key Constituents

Communication among organizational members is the vehicle by which they interact internally as well as externally with stakeholders outside of the organization and is the first role identified by Menefee. Although communication is essential for all personnel within the social work agency, its focus and functions differ for practitioners and administrators in many ways. The primary focus of communication varies along one key dimension: the scope of concern. For practitioners the scope of concern involves clients, whereas for administrators it is the entire agency and its external environment. These interactions may be in person, such as in meetings, or impersonal, such as by telephone, e-mail, or other written correspondence. They take many forms: formal and informal, verbal and nonverbal.

(1) Formal versus Informal Communication

The administrator must understand the use of formal and informal communication in order that each can be used most effectively. Administrators must also recognize that the higher they move up the ladder, the less access they will have to the informal communication system.

We all know that hallway conversation, gatherings at the water fountain, or meetings in the bathroom are where much of the agency action takes place. We also know that much of this communication can be in the form of a gripe session, an opportunity to vent about problems in the organization. However, this area is out of bounds for the administrator, a boundary to be respected.

Martin had just moved up from being a frontline supervisor to managing an entire program. He noticed that when he came into a room, the conversation often stopped. This created a dilemma for Martin, because many of these people were close to him as colleagues over the years. He sensed tension when he attempted to join the conversation. In discussing his feelings of rejection, his supervisor helped him to understand that this was nothing personal, but rather an expected change that occurred in the differentiation of roles.

Thus, much of the administrator's communication is formal and takes place in meetings. It is the administrator's role, and challenge, to effectively design meetings that have several functions: coordinating, distributing work, team building, reporting information, studying a problem, making or ratifying decisions, and monitoring (Brody, 2000). We cannot stress enough the importance of setting an agenda, setting time limits, and keeping the meeting moving. All too often frustration is generated in these formal meetings when the leader abdicates the leadership role of seeing that the goals of the meeting are met as each agenda item is covered, that time limits are respected, and that all are encouraged to participate in the process.

Formal meetings provide an opportunity to introduce opportunities for organizational change and to encourage staff to identify problems that need to be addressed either through internal management or through external advocacy.

In an agency that served welfare recipients it became clear that not only were most jobs for clients available on the night shift but that there was no public transportation to the possible work sites. The supervisor raised the issue at the weekly department meeting and the administrator was able to use this information to advocate with the county commissioners for public vans to meet this particular need.

Formal communication also takes the form of letters, proposals, or reports. Each requires skill in presentation. Administrative writing differs from that of the practitioner in not being detail or process oriented but rather focusing on the goals to be attained and the audience being addressed. Administrators often do not understand the differences in writing style and may require some training to be most effective. For example, the administrator must understand the expectations of the potential funder and write proposals in a rigorous, specific manner. The requirements of foundations as opposed to government agencies must be addressed carefully. Failing to meeting all the requirements can result in a proposal being dropped from consideration.

Ms. Stewart, the CEO of an agency that was rapidly increasing in size to meet new community needs, recognized that she could no longer do the proposal writing for her agency's contracts. However, she had a limited budget and could only use staff from within to do the preliminary work. Ms. Stewart arranged for some training sessions for three of her frontline workers who were interested in having this new challenge but needed help in performing the new task effectively.

A final caveat concerning administrative communication is assuring that communications flow both ways. All too often formal channels of communication are top-down, with top administrators communicating "through a network of key staff people, who in turn communicate with their staff, and so on throughout the organization" (Brody, 2000, p. 280). The hierarchy in such organizations may require policy decisions to trickle down from board or executive levels to frontline workers. Providing clear rationales for changes in policies or programs with explanations as to how workers and clients will benefit from these changes can eliminate confusion or resentment.

However, it is important for all human service organizations to promote the bottom-up flow of communication, and this should be formally structured to assure that frontline workers can communicate changes they observe in their caseloads or problematic public or agency policies that inhibit their ability to provide effective services. This is a form of advocacy that is essential for all workers in the agency, and it is the job of managers to create formal means for accomplishing change based on valuable suggestions offered by workers. It is also important for managers to promote an organizational culture that values input from workers.

(2) Verbal versus Nonverbal Communication

A new lens for understanding the administrative use of nonverbal communication is offered by a focus on the physical environment that communicates the organizational culture to workers as well as clients and other visitors. The physical environment includes posters, floor plans, windows, decor, and notices. Rapp and Poertner report that these symbols "communicate something about the person, the agency, and something about what might occur in the office" (1992, p. 178). An example of one United Way volunteer's experience follows:

John visited a small family service agency in his role as United Way allocations volunteer. He was distressed to see signs everywhere saying "no clients allowed—staff only!" and "clients must provide required paperwork before any services can be given." He visited another agency that was very different. Here he saw posters with ocean and mountain views, positive motivational messages, and a sign saying "this year, we have helped 100 families work toward independence." It was clear to John which agency communicated a welcoming message to clients and visitors.

Rapp and Poertner (1992) further remind us that verbal communications in the client-centered social work agency can be carefully crafted to promote a positive organizational culture. Consider for a moment the differential effect two supervisors would have on workers and, ultimately, clients.

Supervisor 1: Jane, your monthly report was wrong again. Have it on my desk corrected by 4:00 pm.

Supervisor 2: Jane, I thought your report this month was an improvement over last month's; can we talk about ways to improve it further?

Both supervisors are communicating the fact that Jane's report needs work, but Supervisor 1 says it in a way that is both demanding and demeaning, whereas Supervisor 2 says it in a supportive manner. Which supervisor would inspire Jane to provide outstanding services to her clients? Which supervisor would you prefer to work for, and more importantly, which supervisor would you prefer to be?

Boundary-Spanning Roles and Communication

Practitioners typically use limited boundary spanning in their jobs on behalf of their clients, a role identified by Menefee. In contrast, the administrators' role is characterized by extensive boundary spanning both inside and outside the organization as they relate to a variety of individuals and organizations. Not only are they working with other nonprofit agencies that are serving the same consumer group, but they are also in contact with foundations, the media, and government agencies, among others. The types of external communication that are key for administrators include relating the agency's vision, mission, accomplishments, and needs and communicating with other agencies to find ways to collaborate.

The intersection of these two boundary-spanning roles is illustrated by the following case material.

Mr. James was a case manager for a physically challenged consumer. He worked hard in seeking all types of opportunities for his client, including appropriate housing, training, and employment. The biggest obstacle, which he could not address, related to transportation. He brought this to the attention of the agency executive, who proceeded to examine this need from a broader agency perspective, as it affected many of the consumers in the organization. The executive contacted other agencies to mobilize a broader base for addressing the problem.

This outreach is most challenging and requires a new set of communication skills. The use of language becomes very important as different professions and different disciplines have their own special work or jargon. Seeking simple terms that describe the problem that can be universally understood is key; otherwise, new collaborators can be turned off by an insular vocabulary.

The Futurist-Innovator and Communication

The above example also illustrates the Futurist-Innovator role identified by Menefee. Here, the practitioner's role is concerned with observation of trends within the caseload and communicating these to administrators. The administrator supplements this information by communicating with external professionals and understanding the changing environment so the agency can position itself to prepare for buffeting forces.

We wish to emphasize the importance of two other administrative roles cited by Menefee: policy practitioner and advocator. Both are externally oriented but very dependent on the information that has been communicated to them by their staff within the agency. All of these roles require a special commitment and setting of priorities (Perlmutter & Adams, 1994).

The Organizer Role and Communication

The organizer role is relevant in all areas of practice. Whereas the practitioner is client focused, concerned with communicating what the barriers to her or his efforts are to organize caseloads, schedules, and sessions with clients, the administrator is concerned with communication among agency programs to enhance internal coordination in service to effectiveness and efficiency.

Ms. Thomas, the CEO of an employment and training agency, was aware of the competition that existed not only between these two functions of the agency but also among the supervisors who felt that the training side had greater prestige. She began to initiate programs for the staff that would help mitigate these differences and tensions. She spent time focusing on the interdependence of these two programs and the need for greater communication among the staff members. The environment changed dramatically as staff worked together in developing new ideas for external contracts that would support innovative programs.

Evaluation

Evaluation, another role identified by Menefee, is a major responsibility of administration, one that has gained increasing importance as contracts and grants have become a major source of support for the voluntary sector. The administrator must see that the agency evaluates the progress of its clients and communicates service outcomes to stakeholders inside and outside the agency. The amount of time and effort devoted to this task often is viewed by staff as displacing important time that could be used for service delivery. The administrator must be sensitive to the interests and pressures on staff, given that their participation and support of the evaluation process is essential. Therefore, open communication among all parties is essential to maximize cooperation and to reduce conflict.

Of equal importance is the internal evaluation procedure, which focuses on staff performance. The administrator must ensure that the staff evaluation process is one that incorporates both top-down and bottom-up processes. Top-down communication takes place when the supervisor provides feedback on individual employees' job performance.

"Appraisals are an important means of connecting staff performance to the organization's mission and goals. They are useful in focusing on areas requiring staff improvement and training. They contribute to decisions requiring disciplinary action or termination . . . [as well as] . . . salary increases or staff promotions." (Brody, 2000, p. 211)

The performance appraisal process also presents opportunities for bottom-up communication. Here the employee is encouraged to discuss successful resolution of challenges, describe skills acquired, offer suggestions for improvements in client services, and request resources that will enable the worker to be more efficient and effective. In short, performance appraisals provide opportunities for both top-down and bottom-up communication within the agency.

Juanita supervised three case workers in a mental health agency. To her, two were clearly performing their jobs at an outstanding level of effort and effectiveness. The third worker, however, presented Juanita with the challenge of evaluating his poor job performance and deciding if she wanted to retain the worker or give him notice.

Juanita knew the importance of good documentation and began the evaluation meeting with a review of the worker's poor as well as good performance. The common theme for poor performance seemed to be the worker's inability to come to work on time. Because she knew the worker had good case management skills, she decided to explore the reasons for this problem with the worker rather than jump to conclusions.

The worker admitted that he had been having personal problems that he had not wanted to talk about with his supervisor. He had recently taken full custody of his two children and found that his work schedule did not accommodate his responsibilities as a single parent, including transporting them to and from school every day. To make matters worse, his children's school was across town from the work site to which he had been assigned.

Juanita was able to reassign the worker to an agency office that was closer to his children's school and to offer him a flexible work schedule.

Both were pleased with the arrangement, and Juanita was satisfied that by opening the lines of communication she was able to retain a valuable worker to serve the agency's clients.

Supervisor, Facilitator, Team Builder

In one sense, practitioners supervise their clients and must communicate agency expectations and limits to service provision. Similarly, administrators, in these three roles, communicate the vision and mission of the agency to workers at all levels and communicate the value of staff via modeling and reward systems.

Practitioners facilitate the ability of clients to meet their goals and fulfill their needs by informing them of resources that are available from the agency. Similarly, administrators facilitate the ability of workers to do their jobs by understanding and communicating to central administrators the resources needed by workers.

The administrator's role as team builder is to communicate the value of productive teamwork within the agency and to create cooperative teams (for example, coalitions) with other agencies. This is a special skill that requires careful attention (Perlmutter, Bailey, & Netting, 2001). The following case example provides insight into the challenges inherent in this role.

Bill was promoted to supervisor of his work group, and he knew that promoting teamwork among his former coworkers would not be easy. Burnout was a constant threat, and it often emerged in the form of interpersonal conflicts. Determined to improve the work environment and therefore services to clients, he initiated a series of steps designed to improve communication within his work group and with central administration.

Bill started with an open-door policy and encouraged his staff members to present him with regular reports of their accomplishments as well as barriers they encountered to effective service provision. He reorganized his weekly meetings so that they focused on solutions rather than problems. He encouraged the formation of mini-task groups to develop proposals for structural and conceptual changes that he might propose to his supervisors. Each proposal was organized with a problem statement, potential solutions, and identification of resources needed.

Bill recognized the importance of providing feedback to his staff members so they would see the fruits of their labor. Therefore, he promptly forwarded every proposal presented to him to central administrators and just as promptly informed his work group of changes that directly resulted from their suggestions. In short, Bill provided a voice for his staff members, along with feedback, encouragement for individual and group problem solving, and praise.

Within six months Bill and his staff agreed that burnout had been reduced, client services had been improved, and the team-building approach had greatly contributed to a more productive and satisfactory working environment.

A Final Word on the Administrator's Use of Communication

This chapter has presented the many faces of communication within a social work agency for both practitioners and administrators while highlighting the differences in focus and approach for each role. In practice, communication within an organization is pervasive, and the roles do not neatly divide into "yours" and "mine." Effective communication is a competency that the practitioner can expect to hone and improve when moving into an administrative position. Administrators use communication as a tool for accomplishing their aims of program and organizational effectiveness. It is key to their roles as change agents and advocates, both within and outside the agency.

The Administrator and Interorganizational Relations

This chapter examines those professional relationships that must be nurtured across the external boundaries of an agency. In Chapter 3 we presented Menefee's (2000) model of managerial roles, which included that of boundary spanner. Defined as networking and collaboration with external stakeholders to establish and maintain relationships and exchange resources, this role is salient for the discussion of interorganizational relations.

Why Are Interorganizational Relations Important?

The first question to be addressed is the following: Why must managers be concerned with interorganizational relations? Initial theories viewed organizations as closed systems; these have long been replaced by open-systems theories. Hasenfeld emphasizes the importance of the political economy perspective as illustrative of open-systems theory, which "views the organization as a collectivity that has multiple and complex goals, paramount among them, survival and adaptation to the environment" (2000, p. 95). The ability of the organization to survive depends on the mobilization of resources, such as power, legitimacy, money, personnel, and clients (Hasenfeld, 2000). Menefee (2000) further delineates this view: "Establishing interorganizational relations, developing partnerships, and integrating service delivery systems are essential activities for agency survival" (p. 251).

Perlmutter, Bailey, and Netting (2001) present a cogent discussion of strategic alliances that expands our understanding of interorganizational relations.

> Alliance . . . is seen as an umbrella concept under which multiple types of interorganizational relationships can occur. Alliance implies that organizations will want to sustain these relationships, even though they will change over time. These relationships, obviously, take multiple forms and no two are exactly alike. . . . Managerial supervisors will find themselves engaging in these partnerships as they transcend organizational boundaries and interface with other community agencies in order to improve interorganizational collaboration and to reduce duplication of services. (pp. 48–49)

Perlmutter, Bailey, and Netting (2001) provide us with a comprehensive understanding of the importance of building strategic alliances. Reasons for forming alliances include maximizing resource dependence and interdependence; increasing operational efficiency; achieving strategic enhancement; seeking environmental validity; gaining political power; and increasing social responsibility. Each will be described below, with this book's dual themes of change and advocacy highlighted.

Maximizing Resource Dependence and Interdependence

First, by combining existing resources, two or more organizations may be able to achieve their individual or collective goals better than they could working alone. One agency that owns vehicles, some of which are not regularly used, may agree to make them available to another that requires reliable transportation for its clients. Alternately, an agency may outpost a social worker who provides on-site services to clients in another agency; this may result in opportunities to identify clients who could benefit from the agency's other services. These are examples of what Perlmutter, Bailey, and Netting call the "synergistic potential in combining resources" (2001, p. 50).

Second, acquiring and maintaining resources may be achieved via strategic alliances. Brody (2000) identifies financial coordination as a strategy for collaborative structures. This includes joint fundraising, purchase of organizational services, and joint project funding. Contemporary governmental and nongovernmental funders often require collaborative efforts as a prerequisite for financing social services. For example, the U.S. Department of Housing and Urban Development gives 60 points out of 100 for homeless funding applications that are developed by coordinated community service partners. It requires that each community seeking funding develop a continuum of care, defined as "a community plan to organize and deliver housing and services to meet the specific needs of people who are homeless as they move to stable housing and maximum self-sufficiency" (Guide to Continuum, 2001, p. 1).

Increasing Operational Efficiency

Increasing operational efficiency is always an ongoing quest in all social service operations. This includes case management coordination, in which two or more agencies serving the same clients meet regularly to discuss ways to optimize and avoid duplication of services. Managers typically are involved in establishing these relationships via formal or informal interorganizational agreements.

Another means by which alliances attempt to increase operational efficiency are so-called one-stop shops, which are provided "to clients in a geographic area by offering a continuum of services to clients (e.g., child care, child welfare, job training, and medical services) in one location with a single access point" (Perlmutter, Bailey, & Netting, 2001, p. 51). Two examples illustrate one-stop shops offer a continuum of service in which different agencies come together under one roof to provide comprehensive services to their mutual target populations: homeless assistance centers and welfare reform programs.

In Miami, Florida, the Community Partnership for Homeless, Inc., operates two homeless assistance centers. These centers provide centralized intake, short-term residency, food, clothing, showers and beds, case management, adult and vocational classes, job training, legal aid, and child care. The Florida Workforce Investment Act authorizes the development of career centers throughout Florida that provide job search and placement assistance, career counseling, labor market information, assessment of skills and needs, information about available services, follow-up services, comprehensive assessments, development of individual employment plans, group and individual counseling, case management, and short-term prevocational services.

Achieving Strategic Enhancement

A strategic alliance can enhance the organization because it "potentially strengthens the human service organization's position to remain viable in an increasingly competitive service delivery environment by diversifying its funding sources, broadening its client base, and enhancing information and evaluation systems" (Perlmutter et al., 2001, p. 52). For example, links between the public and private sectors have increasingly been encouraged by shifts in governmental trends toward privatization (Gibelman, 2000). Organizational responses include purchase of service contracting, conversion to for-profit status, and the development of formal agreements with managed care networks.

A community mental health center recognized the need to diversify its funding base when state funders indicated that recent budget cuts would likely continue into the future. After assessing the fit between its existing resources (that is, trained counseling staff) and the needs of the private sector, the agency developed a strategy for offering employee assistance programs to local companies. Most small and medium-sized private companies recognized the need for mental health and substance abuse services for their employees but did not have the resources to develop in-house solutions. A win-win solution was developed: the businesses purchased training, education, intervention, and referral services from the community mental health agency, which benefited from the increased revenues that resulted from these purchase-of-service contracts.

Seeking Environmental Validity

Increasing competition among service providers as well as social welfare problems can give rise to imperatives for service delivery strategies that improve credibility among stakeholders. According to Schmid (2000), the "environment provides the organization with the legitimacy . . . it requires for its continued activity" (p. 137). Organizations may rely on other organizations that provide complementary services for human and professional resources that they lack, and alliances can serve to increase the legitimacy of the participating groups. At times, funders mandate interdisciplinary collaboration to reduce service duplication; moreover, commitment to service quality may be demonstrated by an organization's willingness to cooperate with other stakeholders in the community.

Two agencies serving people with physical disabilities in contiguous counties collaborated on a grant proposal for housing and employment services. One agency was well established as a provider of community-based employment programs while the other was recognized for its residential services. The second agency was also smaller and newer than the first. The agencies formed an alliance whereby housing would be provided for the target population in the two counties and clients of the programs would receive employment services throughout the two communities. The first agency benefited from the alliance by identifying a ready referral source for its established and growing employment program; the second benefited by increased legitimacy for its ability to provide comprehensive services.

Gaining Political Power

As we focus on the role of the social work manager as advocate, gaining political power is a strategy that has long been used to enhance political efforts on behalf of clients.

A coalition of agency managers in a New Jersey county met regularly with legislators to provide education and insight into the needs of developmentally disabled citizens. Strategic plans for accomplishing policy advocacy included inviting legislators to visit disability service programs, bringing families and clients to legislators' offices for personal testimonies, organizing large groups to attend legislative hearings on issues affecting clients and services, and sponsoring debates among political candidates.

Thus, political power was gained as the coalition achieved more than any one individual manager could by speaking as one voice and reminding legislators of the huge voting constituencies these agencies represented.

Increasing Social Responsibility

The final rationale for developing strategic alliances is aimed at the role of social welfare organizations in working toward social responsibility. "Specific agency roles are part of an overall programmatic effort with the primary goal of responding to expectations for action in the area of public concerns" (Perlmutter, Bailey, & Netting, 2001, p. 55). Activities related to this role include conducting research in partnership with universities and others and also fostering comprehensive community support for various social problems.

The Substance Abuse Planning and Advisory Boards, which implement programs funded by the Anti-Drug Abuse Act of 1988, is comprised of governmental representatives, social welfare personnel, and citizens, and its goal is to address the myriad of community-level social problems related to substance abuse. This unique alliance brings together people and agencies involved in corrections, prevention, interdiction, and treatment, which are systems that typically do not interact.

Alliances and Advocacy

This discussion emphasizes the importance of building strategic alliances in service of organizational goals related to resources, efficiency, service enhancement, validity, power, and social responsibility. This book's themes of advocacy and change are central to these strategies. First, advocacy efforts for an agency's target population can be enhanced via collaborations with other organizations, whether they are aimed at securing resources for more services or increasing political awareness of client needs. Second, when an organization moves from independence to interdependence, major changes must be managed effectively. Managers need to be aware of, and plan for, resistance among workers because of turf issues, reluctance to relinquish control, and perceptions of increased work burdens. Also, some alliances may require structural changes within the partner agencies. When the benefits of changing to a collaborative model outweigh the costs, managers must anticipate and address resistance to resulting changes if the alliance is to succeed.

Types of Interorganizational Relations

Interorganizational relations occur in various forms, and several models have been developed that describe their structure (for example, Netting, Kettner, & McMurtry, 1998; Perlmutter, Bailey, & Netting, 2001). These models, taken together, describe a range from informal to formal organizational arrangements along a continuum that also takes into account the degree of autonomy of the participating agencies.

Informal Arrangements

Affiliation, the most informal type of arrangement among organizations, is defined as "a loosely connected system of two or more organizations with similar interests" (Perlmutter, Bailey, & Netting, 2001, p. 55). Sharing information or ideas is accomplished via verbal, written, or group processes.

An eight-county community in a large state developed an active Homeless and Hunger Network. The group meets each month to share information about new or changing services, common needs, funding opportunities, and eligibility requirements. The network also provides a forum for comprehensive community planning.

All of the participating agencies retain their full autonomy, thus working together in an informal manner.

Semiformal Arrangements

Next on the continuum, *cooperation* may take place among social service providers or between providers and the private sector. It involves planning and implementing independent programs but also working together toward commonly held goals. Although autonomy of individual participants is maintained, increased formalization via written agreements is common.

A typical example can be found in Information and Referral programs. These programs may involve interagency referrals for services where client eligibility and admissions requirements are specified and known to both agencies. Another example is case conferencing, where workers from two or more agencies meet regularly to discuss clients receiving services from the concerned organizations.

Coordination is another example of a semiformal arrangement, where two or more agencies organize their services to complement each other. These can reduce autonomy for the participating organizations and do require written agreements. The continuum of care approach, discussed earlier, exemplifies coordination as an interorganizational strategy. Coordinated oversight of the community's social service system to monitor service gaps and duplications are typical of these.

Formal Arrangements

Collaboration is the first type of formal arrangement. This occurs when "two or more units within the community agree to set up a new program or service" (Netting, Kettner, & McMurtry, 1998, p. 112). Collaboration usually takes place when one of the partner agencies is unable to provide a specific service on its own, and an exchange of resources makes the program possible. For example, in transitional housing programs for homeless families, day care for children residing at the program is essential. However, the agency providing transitional housing may have space but not fiscal or personnel resources to provide day care services. By collaborating with traditional day care providers, many of these agencies have developed formal contracts for providing services on-site, which is convenient for adult residents who are busy seeking jobs or going to school. In these arrangements, autonomy for both partners is reduced because of the importance of policies and procedures that are acceptable to each.

The second type of formal arrangement is the *federation–association–coalition*. According to Perlmutter, Bailey, and Netting, "The federation/association usually has a staff office to centralize common functions, such as fundraising, public relations, and mission advocacy" (2001, p. 55). Although the member agencies are independent of each other and of the federation, service standards, advocacy positions, and membership fees may be required by the federation.

Examples can be found in state and national organizations, such as United Cerebral Palsy Associations, National Alliance for the Mentally Ill, and the American Cancer Society. Member agencies, although completely autonomous, often adopt a common mission statement and pay dues to the state and national chapters in return for technical assistance, large advocacy efforts, and use of the national identity.

The third form of interorganizational relation is exemplified by *consortia–networks–joint ventures*. These occur when "members of a consortium, a partnership of organizations that identifies itself with a particular interest/issue domain, collectively apply their resources to implement a common strategy and achieve a common goal" (Perlmutter, Bailey, & Netting, 2001, p. 56). These arrangements require legal documents that specify the expectations and responsibilities for joint ownership of shared resources and accomplishment of services and tasks. It is also typical for consortia to develop a joint governance body. For individual partners, autonomy is low in that commonly developed policies and procedures must be followed, but they often retain their central functions of financial and personnel management.

The Homeless and Hunger Network, described previously, determined through cooperative planning that the community needed a comprehensive human services center (CHSC). The network jointly developed a federal proposal to develop this service for homeless and other poor families and individuals. Once funding was secured, plans for the implementation of the joint venture were initiated. The design of the project required each participating agency to provide a service on-site, contribute to the development of policies and procedures to which all service providers would adhere, and identify a representative to sit on the CHSC board of directors. This formal arrangement preserved the autonomy of individual agencies for services provided outside the CHSC but required them to relinquish autonomy (albeit with a vote in policy matters) for services provided within the joint venture.

At the farthest end of the continuum, *mergers–acquisitions–consolidation* represent the most formal arrangement and results in complete loss of autonomy for previously independent agencies. Netting, Kettner, and McMurtry (1998) identify three kinds of mergers:

- horizontal: two agencies consolidate into one organization
- vertical: one large agency absorbs a smaller one
- conglomerate: a large umbrella agency is formed from multiple smaller agencies.

In these instances, "the absorbed organization is completely dissolved and the surviving entity acquires both its assets and liabilities" (Perlmutter, Bailey, & Netting, 2001, p. 57). Clearly, legal documents must be drawn up, often including new bylaws, for this kind of interorganizational arrangement, and the autonomy of the absorbed organization(s) is eliminated.

Mergers can take place when individual agencies find they are in insurmountable competition for resources or when they believe that clients can be better served by formally combined organizations than by those functioning independently. Obviously, managers contemplating mergers must weigh the benefits of improved services and access to resources with the costs of employee morale, client consternation, and community perceptions.

In July of 1997, Parents Anonymous of Maryland and the Child Abuse Prevention Center (CAPC) merged to form The Family Tree. Parents Anonymous and CAPC were small, respected, volunteer-driven agencies headquartered in Baltimore, with complementary programs to prevent child abuse and neglect. Driven by the organizations' desires to reduce competition for funding and to heighten their already strong standings in the community, the merger resulted in a new, even more positive image, a more diverse staff, and the ability to better serve families with an expanded continuum of services. While the merger was successful, The Family Tree has continued to uncover and address the challenges associated with forming unified leadership from two senior staffs and boards of directors, nearly doubling the size of an agency and achieving economies of scale. (Vnenchak & Cronin, 2001, p. 1)

What Is the Manager's Role?

When considering forming a strategic alliance, whether informal or formal, the manager must carefully assess potential positive and negative effects on the agency and its clients. This requires both advocacy and change skills. Pertinent questions include the following:

- Will the alliance increase or reduce the agency's autonomy?
- Will it improve or impair the agency's ability to advocate for individual clients or client groups?
- Is the alliance likely to strengthen or impede the ability of the agency to meet its mission?
- Will the changes that result from the alliance cause resistance or acceptance from key stakeholders, including staff, volunteers, and the public?

Several approaches can assist managers in considering these potential effects on clients and the agency. For example, advisory committees can be helpful in the design and development of any strategic alliance because they can provide legitimacy to the effort. Including clients, client advocates (for example, family members), or both can bring important perspective to advisory committees and further strengthen their perceived legitimacy. Advisory committees require a great investment of administrative time, however, in their selection and structuring. In addition, members must be trained and educated concerning the ongoing requirements of the project.

The cultures of the individual participating organizations must also be examined. There will be similarities and differences in values, constraints, and turf. To ignore these differences is to court disaster.

Administrators bear the responsibility for interpreting the objectives and explaining the proposed alliance to all participating staff members, especially because of the interdependence of all elements in this complex effort. Specifically, how does a particular social worker's role link to the achievement of agency objectives that ultimately deal with meeting consumer needs?

Finally, attention must be paid to the use of incentives, recognition, and rewards. Staff members working at the front line experience great tension and frustration, which often culminate in burnout. Frontline staff members often pay the price for the inconsistencies that take place elsewhere in the system, be it at the policy level, the administrative level, or the client level. An area worthy of special administrative attention is how to help social workers enjoy and be stimulated by the challenges of the new strategic alliance, the merger.

A Successful Merger: A Case Example

In an eight-county area of northern Florida, two HIV/AIDS advocacy organizations struggled to survive separately for several years. One, the HIV/AIDS Prevention Network (HPN), was aimed at prevention and community education. The other, the Panhandle Area HIV/AIDS Network (PAHAN), was concerned with service issues. Both were formed as affiliation alliances with member agencies retaining full autonomy over their respective domains.

Members of both groups recognized the need for change and contemplated a merger. There were several observations that supported this notion. First, participation was declining in both alliances and little was being accomplished to benefit their respective target populations. Second, managers whose agencies spanned the domains of prevention, education, and care were frustrated because they had to attend two separate monthly meetings. Third, several managers were concerned about the seemingly inappropriate dichotomy between prevention and care perspectives. Fourth, federal and state funders were urging agencies in the catchment area to unite. Fifth, planning and funding application processes were, at times, duplicated. Sixth, although PAHAN had a set of bylaws, they were not being followed and the missions of both alliances were not defined. Finally, the eight-county area was eligible for federal funding of coordination efforts, but this money was often returned at the end of the year because it was unused. For these reasons the core group of organizers who were most active in the individual alliances decided to explore the possibility of a merger that would address their concerns.

Although there was agreement among this core group that a merger would have positive outcomes for agencies, clients, and the community, they were concerned about potential negative outcomes. One concern was a possible power imbalance whereby the aims of the prevention advocates would supercede those of care advocates or vice versa, with an overall loss of visibility and legitimacy for the less powerful group. Another concern was the potential loss of input from consumers if the merged organization did not adequately represent their interests. There was a related logistical concern in that HPN tended to meet in the evenings when consumers were more likely to be available, but PAHAN's agency managers preferred to meet during the day. Also voiced was the question of adequate provision of opportunity for representation from among all stakeholders by means of the new structure. Specific to this issue was the fact that both organizations had strong leaders, and identifying one who could lead the new entity was perceived as difficult.

The leader of PAHAN, who maintained the federal allocation for the area, hired a consultant to work toward the following goal: to facilitate a community planning process whereby the members of PAHAN and HPN could develop consensus regarding the benefits and means of merging the two organizations. The consultant initially convened a preplanning meeting with the key leaders of both alliances. At this meeting a strategy was developed that entailed five meetings of a larger group representative of both organizations; the elements of the strategy were the following:

- *identification of common values and goals for HIV/AIDS community activities*
- *development of organizational identity (that is, name), mission, and vision*
- *identification of structural considerations (for example, how the organization will be administered and led; membership issues; and so forth)*
- *planning for implementation (including timeline and assigned responsibilities)*
- *planning for evaluation.*

A group of twelve participants was identified for invitation to subsequent planning meetings. At its first meeting the planning group reviewed the requirements for recognition as a consortium under the Ryan White Care Act to ensure that it encompassed both the prevention and care concerns of member organizations. These included conducting needs assessments, developing plans in concert with the local public health agency, promoting coordination and integration of community resources, assuring the provision of comprehensive services, and evaluating its own effectiveness. Satisfied that the mandate would not prohibit either group from achieving its goals under a merged organization, the consultant next facilitated a discussion of core values common to both. Believing that consensus might not be reached, participants were surprised when they identified core values that were representative of their seemingly diverse perspectives. These were unity, knowledge, acceptance, hope, and service. With this hurdle behind them, they unanimously agreed to merge the two alliances into one.

The planning group made equally rapid progress at the second meeting. The name, vision, and mission statement were all adopted. The new entity, Red Ribbon Alliance, had as its vision "to be recognized as the primary resource for education, information, and advocacy related to HIV/ AIDS in our community." The Red Ribbon Alliance's new mission was "to promote partnerships to identify, secure, and disseminate resources for HIV/AIDS prevention and care efforts in the Big Bend area."

At its next meeting the core planning group was expanded to include all stakeholders from the original two organizations. Collectively, participants decided that the new agency would (1) not be incorporated; (2) ensure open membership with guidelines for voting rights to be defined in a new set of bylaws; (3) invite an impartial organization to serve as the contracted administrator for the Red Ribbon Alliance; (4) develop five committees to address the various elements of the mission statement; (5) ensure that persons living with AIDS have a voice in the alliance; and (6) hold monthly meetings following one more planning session to develop bylaws.

The case example of the Red Ribbon Alliance illustrates many of the concepts presented in this chapter. For instance, forces internal and external to the two original organizations were acknowledged as having potential negative effects on the status quo. Issues of autonomy and formalization were considered, with collaborative planning centered on common concerns used as a strategy to overcome obstacles to change. By achieving consensus on common values of all stakeholders and by working toward mutually agreed-upon goals, the two organizations are positioned to face an uncertain future with a united group of caring advocates.

A Final Word on Interorganizational Relations

This chapter has highlighted the interorganizational elements that must be given priority by the agency administrator. The environment in this discussion is not viewed as context but as organically linked to the internal operations of the agency. It requires proactive leadership. Because an enormous amount of expertise is required, it is essential that the administrator maintain an open and flexible posture, recognizing that the use of experts both inside and outside the agency is appropriate and desirable. Brody comments on the ultimate benefits of strategic alliances for organizations and clients: "Whatever the structural arrangement, collaborative alliances leverage resources to accomplish member agency goals. The synergy that is created by joining together with others results in a greater impact on the clients of the respective agencies" (2000, p. 304).

The Administrator's Work with Volunteers

Volunteers have always played a critical role in human services. Not only have they worked directly with individuals and groups in human service agencies, but they have also been actively involved in policy and governance as members of boards of directors. Although the executives of agencies deal primarily with the board of directors, the work with volunteers (Perlmutter, 1982) is at all levels of the agency and is an important component of administrative responsibility.

Much of the literature in the field of volunteerism focuses on the volunteers themselves, yet it is essential to highlight the administrator's role in providing a structure that makes the volunteer's role not only a productive one but, equally important, a satisfying one.

This chapter opens with a discussion of the various roles of volunteers and moves on to consider the specific challenges for volunteer administration, because social agencies and administrators at all levels are increasingly involved in this newly emerging specialization.

Who Volunteers?

The most familiar historical association with volunteers in the social work profession was with the Charity Organization Societies (COS) and the settlements. At the turn of the 19th century there were friendly

131

visitors who were active with the COS and who stimulated the writings of Mary Richmond; her early thinking about professionalism expressed in *Social Diagnosis* (1917) reflects this movement. The friendly visitors were often wives of board members of charitable organizations and were seen as active service volunteers (Austin, 2000).

There were also the early community activists, such as the young people who moved into urban areas and who participated in the development of the settlement house movement both in England (for example, Toynbee Hall) and the United States (for example, the Henry Street Settlement) (Austin, 2000; DeSchweinitz, 1943; Wald, 1915). They were involved in advocacy and served to influence public policy.

The active involvement of volunteers as direct service providers in the human services was significantly reduced between the 1920s and the 1960s. This change was attributable to several factors. First, social work as a profession emerged and flowered at the turn of the century, and by the 1920s schools of social work were organized and, with the American Association of Schools of Social Work, sought to establish standards for training and practice.

Second, the Great Depression of the 1930s stimulated the active development of the public social service sector, which delivered services through its paid staff. This resulted in a lack of clarity regarding the appropriate use of volunteers and further reduced their involvement as, during the growth of child welfare programs, "a model of professional leadership and professional mentoring developed among the public child welfare workers in many states" (Austin, 2000, p. 36).

Interestingly, many who have chosen social work as a profession entered the field through their experience with volunteering, as high schools and colleges developed service-learning programs throughout the country (Campus Compact, 2000; Gray et al., 1998; Robinson & Barnett, 1996).

The role of volunteers who serve on boards of directors in the nonprofit sector has been rather consistent; they have been continuously involved in this role throughout all these decades and to the present.

A study of the various roles played by volunteers today in the human services challenged the traditional, narrow focus on direct service provision (Perlmutter & Cnaan, 1993). In a study of 470 volunteers who performed direct service, representing 105 human service organizations, the authors found only 3.5 percent of the sample provided direct service only; over two-thirds were also involved in administrative support and advocacy. The authors concluded that, given the fiscal constraints in human services, social work administrators should be creative in redefining and broadening the roles played by volunteers. Given their finding that the pool of potential volunteers consists of more highly educated people, the challenge of an array of policy, advocacy, and administrative roles could enhance recruitment efforts.

This finding is compatible with some important questions that have been raised recently concerning the potential volunteer pool. Austin (2000) observes that today there is "a more careful examination of the diversity of interests represented by the various stakeholder constituencies of nonprofit social welfare organizations" (p. 41) to guard against institutionalized racism and sexism in these agencies. The potential contribution of volunteers to this goal is emphasized by Weinbach: "A volunteer who is also part of the community can provide a kind of legitimization for the organization" (1990, p. 113).

Feminist organizations have raised a different set of issues. Given that women are struggling for economic equality both in opportunity and wages, should they continue in their traditional role as volunteers? Does this not perpetuate a view of women that positions them outside of the economic structure?

These are important sociological and political issues, and administrators must consider them seriously as they seek to recruit potential volunteers. These issues are particularly important as one examines the populations to be served and attempts to match the helpers with those being helped.

Reasons to Volunteer

Why volunteer? This is an important question that must be understood by the administrator who wishes to organize and operate volunteer programs effectively. The motivation is complex and includes both altruistic and individualistic factors. Initially the literature focused on altruism, because service orientations, social change interests, and selflessness were highlighted (Austin, 2000; Ellis & Noyes, 1976; Naylor, 1976; Schindler-Rainman & Lippett, 1977).

Phillips (1984) discusses this from a theoretical perspective. He suggests that social exchange theory, with its interest in costs and benefits, is effective in explaining the impulse to volunteer. In volunteer activities the relationships between the altruistic (cost) and egoistic (reward) motivations are modified by (1) the degree to which the expectations of the volunteer are met (Routh, 1977) and (2) the phase of the volunteer effort (Wolensky, 1980). For example, while the initial motivation to volunteer may be altruistic (that is, to help someone else), that motivation may also be reassessed in terms of the return. Similarly, the decision to continue as a volunteer will be evaluated in terms of its costs and rewards.

It is assumed that altruism is the driving force that stimulates the volunteer to become involved in, for example, college tutoring or head start programs; in spite of this, the phenomenon of volunteer dropout is all too familiar. This behavior is both puzzling and frustrating to the sponsoring agency, and the volunteer is often viewed as lacking maturity and responsibility. However, the volunteer should not necessarily be seen as irresponsible or immature. Often the attrition results from frustration with the task at hand. For example, if children being helped are erratic in their attendance (a pattern that the volunteers tend to view as their own failure), the volunteers need to be helped to understand, accept, and even expect this to happen as a reality of the program.

This situation is confirmed by a large national study of the public, which found that citizens often stop volunteering because of poor volunteer management practices (United Parcel Service Foundation, 1998). Too often, when the agency has not provided the appropriate supervision or support the volunteers need to understand the populations being helped or their special interests and needs, it is easier for the agency to blame the victim (that is, the volunteer) rather than examine its own role in the problem. For example, if child absenteeism is discussed and interpreted in terms of the helper's realities and not as a failure of the volunteer and if volunteers are helped to develop new strategies for outreach, the volunteers would be both empowered and recognized for their efforts.

As a result, attention has been paid more recently to the needs of the volunteers themselves. Weinbach (1990) notes such motivations as education, intellectual stimulation, social interaction, seeking responsibility, and sharing skills. Furthermore, volunteers tend to get discouraged when there is little feedback about the effectiveness of the activity or the quality of performance on the part of the volunteer. This can be readily corrected by the agency. In terms of the social exchange theory cited previously, without this supervisory support the costs to the volunteers far exceed the rewards. Not surprisingly, this leads to dropping out.

The rewards of volunteering were poignantly captured by one individual who worked for seven years on a community hotline (described in more detail in the following section).

"When I started here way back in the day as a volunteer for 2-1-1 BigBend, I had no idea that it would change my life forever. I thank 2-1-1 BigBend for teaching me an abundance of communication and counseling skills that have seemed to serve me in every aspect of my life. I also thank 2-1-1 BigBend for exposing me to people of all different backgrounds and lifestyles and teaching me to appreciate those differences. I thank 2-1-1 BigBend for providing me with an environment to grow and learn the talents I never knew I had. Most of all, I thank 2-1-1 BigBend for supporting me and treating me like family. Even though I am excited about moving into a new career, I will truly miss the time I had here." (2-1-1 BigBend, 2002, p. 2)

Organizational and Professional Controls in Volunteer Programs

The protection of the client and the maintenance of professional standards are of great importance in all social service agencies; consequently, in defining the role of the nonprofessional, the conscious differentiation between organizational and professional controls is crucial. To this end it is useful to examine the factors that can help structure a volunteer experience as one examines the organizational and professional controls that are important for successfully integrating volunteers into the work of the agency.

The *organizational controls* are defined by and occur within the structure of the agency, whereas the *professional controls* reside with the volunteer and are the product of professional training and experience. If one serves on the board of directors because of legal or financial expertise, clearly the professional controls inform that role. By contrast, if a high school student is a big sister or big brother to a young child, then the organizational controls come into play to offer a framework for effective performance (for example, defining the nature of the activity, limiting the personal contact, and so forth).

Regardless of the level of involvement the professional staff must attempt to give the volunteers an understanding of their roles and an understanding of the goals of the organizational setting.

Two Case Examples of Organizational and Professional Controls

Volunteers can fulfill limited or extensive roles in social work organizations. Limited roles can range from participation in fundraising events, such as walks or runs for charity, to serving meals at homeless shelters or sponsoring an annual picnic for abused children. Extensive roles include those in which volunteers are essential for the accomplishment of the agency's mission and generally require considerable organizational and professional controls. Two case examples of the latter are presented below.

Case 1: Guardian Ad Litem Programs

The very mission of Guardian Ad Litem Programs is oriented toward volunteers: "to recruit, train, support and supervise volunteers to advocate for the best interest of children who are alleged to be abused, neglected, or abandoned and who are involved in court proceedings" (Guardian Ad Litem, 2002, p. 1). The lay volunteer model is used in many states, with legal standards established for the operation of the programs. Programs have professional staff members who recruit, train, supervise, and assist volunteers and have attorneys who provide legal expertise.

Guardian Ad Litem volunteers (GALs) perform a variety of intensive services. These include investigating cases of alleged abuse by interviewing all relevant parties (including the child, parents, relatives, friends, and teachers); monitoring agencies and others responsible for providing services; observing children's interactions with family members; preparing reports for case files and court records; coordinating services needed by the children; and representing the children's interests in court hearings.

Similarly, the commitment expected of GALs is considerable. Volunteers are expected to devote between 2 and 10 hours per week to their cases and are required to attend both preservice and in-service training sessions, with a minimum of 6 hours per year of in-service training required to maintain ongoing certification as a GAL.

Both organizational and professional controls are present in this case. By providing legislative authority for GALs as well as training and close supervision, the organization ensures that the work of lay volunteers is consistent with and in service to the needs of both legal and ethical mandates for the care of vulnerable children. Professional controls are represented by the identification of three pre-existing qualities needed by all volunteers: capability for helping a child in crisis, time, and caring.

Case 2: 2-1-1 BigBend

2-1-1 BigBend is an agency that relies on its volunteers to staff its hotlines. These volunteers provide local counseling and referrals, statewide HIV/ AIDS information and counseling, local after-school support for children, and family health support. The hotlines receive approximately 39,000 calls per year, a staggering number that represents the critical need for volunteers. These volunteers are supervised and trained by paid professional staff members.

All volunteers are required to be at least 18 years of age and to attend 75 hours of training. In addition, volunteers are expected to commit to 200 hours of volunteer time per year, with further specifications for three three-hour shifts and one overnight shift each month. All prospective volunteers are interviewed before acceptance into the program, with the qualities of caring and bilingual expertise actively sought through this process.

2-1-1 BigBend emphasizes the rewards as well as the commitment expected for its volunteers. The rewards include personal growth, building interpersonal skills, networking opportunities, work–study and internship opportunities, and course credits from the local university. Also, the agency regularly recognizes its volunteers through two vehicles: counselor of the month and volunteer and staff appreciation banquets.

Organizational controls exemplified by this case include training requirements and the provision of professional staff oversight. Professional controls arise from the experiences that volunteers bring to the role of hotline worker as well as those they develop through their hotline work and training.

Although volunteers can serve in most, if not all, roles within social welfare organizations, Weinbach (1990) warns that there are potential costs and dangers to their involvement. For example, they may be more difficult to control because they do not need to work in the organization, that is, their performance is not tied to job retention. In addition, as nonprofessionals they may not share the values or ethical imperatives held by paid staff; punctuality and confidentiality exemplify these concerns. Accordingly, Rapp & Poertner (1992) recommend that "before seeking volunteers, the organization must examine its needs and determine the types of expertise that it will require from volunteers" (p. 236).

What Is the Field of Volunteer Administration?

The field of volunteer administration is broad and exists in an array of settings, both public and private. These include hospitals, churches, scouting movements, settlement houses, programs for developmentally disabled individuals, mental health settings, child welfare agencies, services to the aging, and correctional programs, among others.

Administrators of volunteer programs are both paid and unpaid, an indicator of the formative stage of this emerging profession (Perlmutter, 1984). The unpaid status is clearly linked to the historical role of women as unpaid volunteers, as illustrated by the arguments put forth by Braithwaite as early as 1938. First, she cites the value to the volunteer in that the role provides "valuable training for citizenship." Second, and of particular relevance to the above-mentioned argument raised by the feminist movement, there are many capable female administrators who would not stand a chance at being elected to public office on local government bodies but who have the expertise regarding social service as well as "more time to devote to the work." Third, the capacity for the public sector to hire "administrative personnel qualitatively and quantitatively is limited, and yet, there are many public spirited people [who] have specialized public interests and specialized experience—they would willingly serve as administrators of, for example, hospitals or housing" on a voluntary basis (pp. 57–59).

The backgrounds of these paid and unpaid administrators of volunteer programs also vary in terms of both education and experience. Usually the person comes up through the ranks and operates on an idiosyncratic, ad hoc basis. Although this process provides an opportunity for the creative individual with administrative proclivities to emerge and provides recognition of these abilities, the person usually operates in isolation and in a vacuum, all too often feeling unsupported in the sponsoring organization.

Most of the people now employed as volunteer administrators work alone or with very few associates who understand what conflicting pressures can build up. To survive, volunteer administrators must walk a fine line between administrative pressures to pick up a miscellany of tasks with community relations aspects and community pressures to serve the purposes of individuals or groups. Clarity about values and also great skill are required to bring all goals into congruence with the idea of service to meet the real needs of persons for whom the services are intended.

What Do Administrators of Volunteer Programs Do?

Rapp & Poertner (1992) observe that "depending upon the size of the agency, the volunteer program may be informal, involving only a few people, or it may be highly organized with staff directing and coordinating the work of volunteers" (pp. 236–237). Even small volunteer programs require the designation of a professional for supervision (Weinbach, 1990). The role of the administrator of a volunteer program is often ill-defined and amorphous. It spans an array of administrative tasks that encompass both middle-management and top-management functions.

The administrator of volunteer programs is perceived as being primarily involved in the more widely known tasks of recruitment and placement. However, these two aspects are only part of what should be considered a total approach to personnel or human resources management. Other functions include staff development, in-service training, and supervision. They are designed to ensure effective and satisfying performance on the part of the volunteer.

The Association for Volunteer Administration (1999) has identified many other professional roles of the volunteer administrator, which are comparable to the role of the social work administrator:

- assessing the need for volunteers
- developing a compelling vision and mission for the volunteer program
- generating a plan for implementing the volunteer program
- developing and managing the program budget
- creating volunteer position descriptions
- developing policies and procedures aimed at safety for volunteers, paid workers, and clients
- recruiting, interviewing, and placing volunteers
- orienting and training volunteers
- fostering partnerships among paid and unpaid staff in the organization
- monitoring the work of volunteers
- maintaining volunteer participation records
- evaluating outcomes of the volunteer program
- recognizing efforts of volunteers
- dismissing volunteers whose performance is unsatisfactory
- advocating for volunteerism.

Thus, many technical areas of performance are similar to those performed by social work administrators in a wide array of settings. It is also clear that the administrator of volunteer programs faces some unique challenges.

The social work profession can provide an appropriate base for this essential professional development because of the many areas of compatibility between the profession of social work and the field of volunteerism. First, and perhaps foremost, is the concern of both fields with advocacy, an important thrust articulated in the 1970s (Manser & Cass, 1976).

> The possibilities for strengthening programs . . . are growing out of experience in community action programs and governmental services as well as more traditional voluntary agencies. Acting as advocates volunteers serve clients directly, help people find appropriate services, or mobilize resources in their behalf. (Naylor, 1976, p. 12)

The importance of the advocacy role of volunteers on advisory boards, self-help groups, and citizen boards required by program funders has been equally noted (Lewis, Lewis, & Souflée, 1991; Rapp & Poertner, 1992; Weinbach, 1990).

A second area of compatibility between volunteerism and social work can be found in the fact that both are practiced in a broad array of settings and fields of service. These include organizations focused on the environment, civil rights, culture, education, health care, communities, politics, recreation, religion, and service clubs. Third, many social service agencies, such as homes for the aged, hospitals, or feminist agencies, already have large volunteer programs; this could allow for the development of fieldwork internships in volunteer administration as part of professional social work training. Fourth, the administrative role of change agent depends in large part upon volunteers on the board of directors for its success, who must consider and approve both large-scale (such as the mission) and small-scale (such as policies) change efforts. Finally, social administration is practiced at both the middle-management and top-management levels; consequently, the administrative skills necessary for volunteer administration are also part of the expertise that is provided in MSW programs with specializations in administration.

It must also be noted that the social work administrator is in a unique position to contribute to the effective development and utilization of volunteers. The social work administrator has the added possibility of defining the roles, interpreting the functions, and bridging the gap between the volunteers and the professionals.

A Final Word on the Administrator's Work with Volunteers

Volunteers provide an important human resource in the provision of social service. Their activities complement the functions of professionals. It is the administrators of these programs who must serve the critical role of providing a structure to help the volunteers function to the utmost of their capabilities and to structure the roles and relationships between the professionals and the volunteers.

The field of volunteer administration is struggling to establish a professional identity. This is evident from a broad array of activities: new professional journals are being published and professional associations are becoming active in providing leadership, guidance, and research (for example, The Association for Volunteer Administration and Association for Research on Nonprofit Organizations and Volunteer Action). Nonetheless, the status of volunteer administration as a profession remains vulnerable today. Given that volunteers are an important human resource in social service, it is important that they be considered in this volume, for it enriches the discussion of the field of social work administration and illustrates an important area of initiative for innovative administrators.

The opportunities are exciting for the social work administrator who seeks to serve populations in need in meaningful ways, not only in the effective provision of service and advocacy but also in helping to shape this new administrative identity, that of administrator of volunteer programs.

Obtaining and Administering Financial Resources

Garnering financial resources is a central concern of all institutions in American society and is a primary responsibility of the social work administrator. This includes both obtaining and managing the resources. The ability to handle this function is vital for administrative effectiveness, and is included as a primary activity in Table 1-1.

This chapter discusses some of the critical administrative issues related to financial resources. We will begin with a focus on obtaining the resources and then consider the management of these resources.

Obtaining Financial Resources

From the inception of the voluntary sector, resource mobilization has commanded attention among social service agencies as they struggled for fiscal survival. In earlier years individual agencies had little hope of attracting support from beyond their own constituencies. Wealthy board members and their contacts were the primary sources of funds.

The advent of community-based United Way agencies in the early 20th century consolidated fund-raising activities in the voluntary sector. Several fundamental changes occurred. For instance, donors were separated from the services that their money supported, creating a less personal relationship between the donor and the recipient organization. Thus, while retaining responsibility for their own agencies' fiscal solvency, the boards of directors of individual agencies became removed from fund-raising activities.

All this activity took place in the nonprofit sector. Federal funds were not available for private agencies until the 1960s. At that time the federal government made a complete about-face from its clearly defined position of noninvolvement with the voluntary sector. An extensive pattern of public funding developed in the forms of grants, contracts, and purchase of services that nurtured and supported the voluntary sector for almost two decades. New needs were identified, new structures were developed, new populations were served, and new expectations emerged.

Administrators became central figures in this function for the first time, with responsibilities for decision making concerning how to obtain funding. This is not surprising, as the skills necessary to obtain funds became based on professional expertise, in contrast to the earlier use of personal contacts. Proposal writing also became a major administrative activity.

Because there was little experience up to the late 1960s to guide administrators or agency boards in the use of public funds, the challenge was to establish new relationships between the nonprofit and public sector. Neither administrators nor boards of directors realized that it was no longer merely a question of obtaining funds or seeing that the books were balanced. They overlooked the importance of understanding the relationship between the public policy intent and the voluntary agency purpose. Discussions began to appear in the professional literature concerning public–private relationships (Austin, 2000; Family Service of America, 1960; Selig et al., 1963), and contracting for services was the primary mechanism for formalizing government and private ventures (Martin, 2001).

A central issue that was raised in the 1960s and that remains important today is whether the private agency can retain its autonomy if it accepts public funds. Will agency policy be determined by the government because of its financial and other stipulations? Is there a relationship between the amount of money accepted and agency policy?

An early national study (Perlmutter, 1971) showed that voluntary agencies can retain their autonomy if they are clear about their objectives, their system's requirements, and their selection of public funds. Otherwise, the available public funds could serve to stimulate unplanned and irrational agency growth that would leave social service agencies without an independent basis for stability. These findings, which are still relevant, reflect what is grist for the administrator's mill today.

The shift in the federal government's posture with respect to social welfare had its origins in the Nixon administration, as a reduction in the funding and number of federal programs became the clarion call (Austin, 2000). Full-scale implementation of this new philosophy did not occur, however, until the 1980s, under Ronald Reagan.

The voluntary sector, which had been accustomed to two decades of program expansion stimulated by federal social policies and programs, faced dramatic cutbacks in that decade. Much of the professional literature of the period dealt with cutback management, because the administrative challenge was to do more with less (Austin, 2000; Finch, 1982; Lohmann, 1984; Randall, 1979). The administrative role shifted to that of financial entrepreneurship, marketing, and contract management.

The watchword of the 1990s was devolution, the shifting of power from a central government to the states. The effect of devolution on social services was that major restrictions were placed on how welfare funds could be spent. The ripple effect could be felt throughout the entire social service delivery system as agencies experienced reductions in government funding for an array of services, including child care, counseling, job training and placement, and health care.

The Personal Responsibility and Work Opportunity Act of 1996, with its elimination of entitlement programs, forced agencies, their administrators, and boards of directors to carefully consider their ability to serve their traditional target populations. The intent of the George W. Bush administration to fund faith-based organizations adds further complexity to the picture (Cnaan, with Boddie, Handy, Yancey, & Schneider, 2002; Cnaan & Boddie, 2002; Wineburg, 2001).

New Approaches to Obtaining Financial Resources

The ultimate outcome of these trends on the funding of social services in the new millennium is increased competition. Traditional nonprofit social service agencies are facing competition from the for-profit sector, from faith-based organizations, and from government and quasi-government entities. Social work administrators have begun to recognize the existence and potential influence of competition and have begun to develop and implement innovative strategies for the very survival of their agencies. These strategies include funding diversification, privatization, collaborative fundraising, cause-related marketing, for-profit ventures, and fees for service.

(1) Funding Diversification

Diversification of a nonprofit agency's funding base can provide stability and can decrease resource dependency (Gibelman, 2003). This supports the old adage, you should never put all your eggs in one basket.

Executives are beginning to recognize the importance of actively seeking funding from an array of sources, including government contracts, United Way and other community funds, private and corporate donations, foundation grants, endowment proceeds, or managed care contracts (Ezell, 2000). Although diversified funding can increase an agency's ability to survive, this strategy requires considerable managerial expertise in such skills as bidding, reporting, regulatory compliance, and performance measurement.

Furthermore, managers often find that various funders have differing fiscal years, which complicates the budgeting and auditing process. Difficult decisions must be made regarding the agency's target population, especially when only a portion of the agency's client base is determined to be eligible for services by some funders. Similar challenges are experienced when individual funders will reimburse the agency for specific services provided only by staff members with specific credentials (for example, a psychiatrist must be specified as providing service traditionally provided by social workers).

Finally, administrators and boards of directors must carefully weigh the possibility that a diversity of funding sources may dilute the mission of the organization. Questions of autonomy raised earlier in this chapter are relevant to this concern and must be balanced with the stability offered by a diversified funding base.

(2) Privatization

Privatization has stirred concern in various quarters, ranging from small-business interest groups to federal and state policymakers. Austin (2000) describes its development:

> The commercialization of health care and mental health care services began with private employer health insurance contracts, but it was then extended to government-funded mental health services and Medicaid-funded medical services. The process of privatization was also extended in many states to include publicly funded child welfare services of many types. (p. 40)

Defined as "divesting government of the responsibility for the funding and provision of products or services" (Gibelman, 2003, p. 26), privatization has resulted from the emphasis on nongovernmental solutions to social problems. For example, state welfare reform-related service systems are increasingly subsumed within larger workforce development efforts based in the private sector. In these environments nonprofit organizations must develop partnerships with previously unknown entities to successfully compete for service contracts. Furthermore, administrators are placed in the position of advocating for social service needs that often take second place in the context of statewide economic development.

(3) Collaborative Fundraising

Collaborative fundraising can take place on a large or small scale. The efforts of large-scale community funds, such as United Way, Women's Way, or Black United Fund, involve a set of constraints including increased reporting and fiscal management requirements;

expectations for speaking engagements on behalf of the federation; and adherence to blackout periods when individual agencies may not conduct fundraising activities during the federated appeal period.

A more recently emerging approach to fundraising that differs from the large-scale community funds is the collaboration of two or more agencies to jointly plan, market, and conduct a fundraising activity, such as a concert or mail campaign. They then share the proceeds. For small projects, considerations include the portion of effort versus the proportion of proceeds; the possibility that public perceptions of worth and legitimacy differ for the two organizations; questions of autonomy; and the potential for the blurring of each participating agency's individual mission.

There are challenges for the social administrator when considering participation in either small or large federated fundraising activities. Thus, what seems on the surface to be a simple means of attracting new resources to an agency must be critically examined for the potential effects, both positive and negative, on the organization. This requires proactive leadership skills on the part of administrators and effective joint decision making with the board of directors.

(4) Cause-Related Marketing

Cause-related marketing, also known as commercial coventures, "is based on a relationship between a corporate sponsor and a charitable organization" (Gibelman, 2003, p. 47). The key element in these arrangements is that it is clearly understood that both the commercial and nonprofit entities will realize profits from the venture. Cause-related marketing may involve donation of proceeds from the sale of a service or product to a charity, underwriting the cost of a charity event in exchange for publicity, or use of a charity's name and logo on a company's product via a licensing agreement (Gibelman, 2003). An example of cause-related marketing is the mutually beneficial partnership between Tyson Foods, Inc., and Share Our Strength.

In May 2000, two Tyson Foods' tractor-trailers, containing 65,000 pounds of chicken, traveled from northwest Arkansas to Chicago to launch the

*company's three-year, $10 million commitment to fight hunger in part-
nership with Share Our Strength, a national anti-hunger organization.
Upon arrival the chicken was donated to hunger relief efforts in the Chicago area.*

*With a limited supply of protein at food banks across the country, Tyson
Foods, Inc., the nation's largest producer and marketer of poultry, provides a much-needed product in the fight to alleviate hunger and malnu-
trition. In addition, it is able to lend powerful marketing mechanisms, a
nationwide distribution system, and employees from facilities around the
country to the cause.*

*Share Our Strength supports nationwide food assistance and education
programs and each year mobilizes thousands of individuals to organize
events, host dinners, teach cooking and nutrition classes, and serve as anti-
hunger advocates. In an effort to sustain these activities the organization
maintains a strong commitment to creating community wealth—resources
generated through profitable enterprise, such as cause-related marketing
partnerships—to promote social change (Tyson Foods, 2003, p. 1).*

The ethical dilemmas inherent in such arrangements must be taken
into account by administrators who consider them. What are the costs
of aligning a charity with a corporation that has questionable business dealings? Should proceeds be accepted from companies that produce goods that are harmful to the agency's target population? Will
the commercial entity expect recognition beyond that specified in
licensing agreements? These and other questions must be faced and
answered before accepting cause-related marketing as a viable source
of financial support for nonprofit organizations.

(5) For-Profit Ventures

Today the voluntary social welfare sector is the subject of a critical
policy debate that focuses on its tax-exempt status. Not only has the
Internal Revenue Service increased its expectations of accountability
for nonprofits with regard to its for-profit ventures, but legislation
also has been passed that requires that for-profit ventures support the
mission of the social agency or else their for-profit status, used as an

organizational strategy for earnings, will be taxed. Thus, a series of criteria for the profit-making venture, which must be met to have a tax-exempt status, have been articulated by several states.

In addition, there have been conversions from nonprofits responding to the privatization environment. Yet Gibelman (2000) warns us of negative outcomes for investor-owned social welfare agencies, such as "the potential for inappropriate, aggressive marketing and pricing strategies to achieve financial gain" (p. 129). Clearly, the mission of the for-profit organization is aimed toward profitability, which can easily subsume client service-oriented goals. This quagmire is no less a concern, however, for nonprofit organizations that are competing for declining financial resources; when an agency seeks new funding to support its efforts to survive but is not consistent with its mission, there is the danger that goal displacement may result.

The thesis here is that venturing activity is not just another resource development strategy designed to broaden the resource base of social service. Venturing activity shifts the decision-making process from a routine management concern with resource development to a critical management decision (Selznick, 1957) with long-range and, possibly, unanticipated consequences that could transform not only the agency but also the voluntary social welfare sector. This was a danger identified by Perlmutter and Adams (1990) in their study of the consequences of venturing activity in a mental hospital. Riverview Rehabilitation Center provides a case study of heuristic value that highlights some of the dilemmas.

Riverview's mission had two components: serving the poor and working in the medical arena. In responses to changes in the medical field over the years, the institution shifted from its original focus on tuberculosis to alcoholism and, finally, to drug and alcohol addiction. Thus, the treatment orientation has always remained central, consistently serving the poor.

In the 1980s, a dilemma arose when it was clear that Riverview could not survive if it continued to serve only the medically indigent who were supported by medical assistance. Because Riverview was forced to find new fiscal mechanisms for survival, the board of directors responded by broadening the definition of client eligibility to include those who were not poor.

The board was clearly committed to protecting the original population, but it saw the expansion as a necessity. By allocating about 30 percent of its beds to paying clients, it was able to accomplish this objective.

With this shift, however, it became clear that the hospital had begun to shed its image as an institution for the indigent. Indeed, a new element entered into the equation as Riverview moved into commercial activity.

Nonprofit organizations that venture into commercial activities usually engage in this new function to support a traditional program that is no longer financially secure by generating revenues in new ways. However, a national study of commercial venturing of nonprofits found that the profits that were anticipated were not realized and that the costs of mounting a for-profit venture were greater than anticipated (Adams and Perlmutter, 1991).

(6) Fees for service: not a new strategy

Although nonprofit organizations have offered services on the basis of sliding-scale fees for many years, variations on this practice have emerged. Managed-care companies that provide funding for service agencies often require copayments from clients that are not related to their ability to pay , or agencies may choose to change their target populations to those who can pay for their own care. This new development must be carefully evaluated in terms of its effect on the people being served.

Preliminary research on the consequences of fees for service and other profit-making ventures on nonprofit voluntary agencies suggests that an unanticipated consequence can be a shift or a dramatic alteration of the traditional social service agency. What may emerge is a system in which the decision-making process is removed from the hands of the traditional actors (for example, clients, boards, professionals) and placed in the hands of third-party payers whose stake is fiscal efficiency rather than service effectiveness. Given the surge in interest in profit-making ventures among nonprofit social agencies, it becomes essential to critically examine this phenomenon, its applications, and its implications.

Administering Financial Resources: Budgeting and Fiscal Accountability

Executives have ultimate responsibility for the financial acumen of their agency's financial performance. Their role will vary depending on the size of the agency and the extent of the support staff available. In a small agency the executive will handle the budget, whereas in a large agency a financial officer will do the hands-on work. In either case it is the executive who must ensure that the books are in order, that the budget is balanced. Social work organizations have a tremendous obligation for fiscal accountability to all of the funders, including private donors, foundations, government grants, and so on.

Effective management of social service organizations' financial resources is increasingly important because of several trends: growth of agency budgets, increasing demands for productivity and accountability, competition with other service providers, and the emergence of managed care funding mechanisms. It falls on the shoulders of the social work administrator to adopt a financial management perspective that "represents another way of looking at the operations of a human service agency or program" (Martin, 2001, p. 7). The essential feature of sound financial management is its emphasis on control of cash, funds, costs, and accounts (Martin, 2001).

The effective administrator will design organizational structures to balance the polarized imperatives of client and funder needs. In other words, while it may make sense to define programs or service activities by the types of clients served and their needs, it is equally important to consider limitations imposed by funding sources. For example, an administrator may want to organize all children's services into one department; however, the primary funders of these services may have limitations placed on the types of children's services they will fund. The result is often what appears to be a hodge-podge of service configurations, with children's recreational services in one department and children's counseling services in another.

There are other, more technical considerations for the administrator with financial responsibilities. For example, in small agencies with flat hierarchies the administrator may function as the chief financial officer of the organization, in which case she or he will need to have many specific skills: understanding how to produce financial statements for review by an auditor, how to read audits, and how to prepare tax returns. On a day-to-day basis the administrator must know how to record revenues and expenses and must understand such accounting terms as accruals, assets, and liabilities, to name a few. Similarly, administrators must understand the reasoning behind internal control systems.

A major stakeholder of the financial operation is the board of directors. Administrators are responsible for regularly reporting factual accounts of the organization's financial position, including cash availability, the likelihood of meeting payroll obligations, and the status of investments. It is clear that this requires more than a rudimentary understanding of financial operations, and the administrator's job may be in jeopardy if he or she does not accurately and regularly provide financial information to the board of directors. This is especially true if there has been any malfeasance in the administration of financial resources.

In very large agencies some of these challenges are eliminated, but others are created. The need for in-depth knowledge about accounting practices and principles may shift from the shoulders of the social work administrator to those of the chief financial officer or to certified public accountants who work as internal auditors, thus relieving part of the burden for the administrator. However, the more people involved in financial management, the more chance something will go wrong; therefore, controls must be put in place for double-checking the books. Even when there are certified accountants on staff to handle these duties, it is still the ultimate responsibility of the social work administrator to ensure that the agency's resources are secure. Thus, strategies for ensuring the protection of the agency's assets must be employed; these can include attending workshops on financial management or recruiting one or more accountants to the board of directors to assist in the oversight function.

The primary vehicle for internal control of financial resources is the budget. This represents the fiscal plan for the coming year and should be viewed as at least as important a priority as a service plan.

Administrators must have a working understanding of the budget process, budgeting cycles, and budget oversight. It is highly recommended that administrators use a bottom-up approach to the budgeting process whereby direct care workers, middle managers, and even support staff are consulted for their perception of the fiscal resources they need to do their jobs effectively and efficiently. In this way the administrator can plan to match service needs with financial resources.

External control of financial resources is as important as internal controls. The typical mechanism used for this purpose is the independent audit. An independent audit is required for any nonfederal organization that receives more than $300,000 of federal funding per year (Ezell, 2000). An independent auditor "is one who is not an internal auditor and one who is not involved in either creating the financial accounting practices of a human service agency . . . or maintaining the agency's financial books and records" (Martin, 2002, p. 201).

The administrator is not relieved of responsibility for the soundness of the agency's fiscal operation just because there is an external, independent audit prepared each year. On the contrary, the process of preparing for an audit and selecting an independent auditor is key to effective financial management and requires specialized administrative skills. First, recognizing that time is money is important: auditors charge organizations by the hour and when the internal bookkeeping system is organized and complete, the expenses associated with the external auditing process can be minimized. Put simply, if the auditors arrive at the agency and find the books in disarray, improper accounting practices, or questionable internal controls, it will take them longer to sort out the mess and will cost the agency more money. Of course, money spent on auditors can mean less money available for client services. Second, the importance of the auditor selection process should not be understated. "Human service administrators need to exercise care when selecting an external CPA or CPA firm to conduct an audit" (Martin, 2002, p. 207). The auditing firm must have a thorough understanding of generally accepted government auditing standards, including the unique expectations for agencies receiving federal and state funds. The selection process, therefore, is critical, and it includes a bidding process whereby several auditing firms are invited to submit proposals that describe their experience auditing social service organizations, estimated costs, and references. The agency administrator will select among these bids and present those that best match the needs of the agency to the board of directors, which has ultimate responsibility for approving the best prospect for the job.

Other skills required of the administrator include forecasting and fee setting. Both are linked with service provision. Forecasting involves planning for resources that will be needed in the future to meet anticipated changes in service configurations. Fee setting is an important process that balances the ability of clients to contribute to the cost of services with the need for fees to supplement or supplant dwindling public funding. Also, in a managed care environment, fee schedules must be carefully designed to provide sufficient revenues to support operations without costing the agency out of the competition.

Although the prospective administrator may be put off by a bewildering array of technical terms used in discussions about financial management, it may be helpful to keep in mind that "human service administrators do not have to give up something (e.g., the client perspective) in order to adopt a financial management perspective" (Martin, 2001, p. 7). Rather, administrators can take comfort in the knowledge that the new set of skills they develop will ultimately contribute to the organization's ability to provide services to those in need.

A Final Word on Obtaining and Administering Financial Resources

This overview of the changing history of obtaining financial resources as well as the administrative responsibility for the budgeting process is intended to help the reader understand the centrality of this activity in the work of the agency administrator. This challenging and stimulating area is full of *sturm und drang*. But it is also an opportunity for creative leadership, provided it is based on careful analysis, skillful planning, and the involvement of appropriate actors in the agency's internal and external systems.

Gummer (1990) provides us with a hopeful perspective: "Rather than viewing declining resources as a constraint requiring a rational and systematic approach to reducing agency operations, many administrators will view it as a challenge to their abilities to capture new resources and preserve existing ones" (p. 65).

CHAPTER 12
Administering Alternative Social Service Agencies

The 21st century has been ushered in at a time of conservatism. The diverse needs of populations at risk often are not met, be they, for example, in health care, housing, or employment. This situation is further compounded by the fact that the public sector is cutting back its provision of human services and support for these services. It becomes all the more urgent to explore new approaches to dealing with social problems, many of which are not of interest to the broader community.

The experience of alternative social agencies, a phenomenon of the 1970s and 1980s, can offer insights into nontraditional responses to the situation. It therefore becomes useful to revisit the experience of that new type of human service organization.

Although special attention must be paid to the role of all the people involved, including the organizers, board members, staff, and consumers, of particular relevance for this volume are the executives who administer these programs. While technical skills used by all administrators are important, this discussion highlights the unique and overarching requisites inherent in alternative social service organizations that require special leadership skills.

This chapter begins with a discussion of the characteristics of alternative social service agencies and applies them to a case study. The chapter concludes with a consideration of the implications of these new agencies for administrative practice.

Understanding Alternative Organizations

The existence of a variety of unsolved social problems has always served as a stimulus for the creation of voluntary social service agencies when the treatment of these problems and the responses to them appeared to be both pressing and possible. The founders of these services, with the élan of a social movement, took the situation into their own hands to rectify inequities in society at large. The literature from those early, heady days still provides the best analysis of that experience.

Although there are many similarities between traditional social service agencies and alternative agencies, Grossman and Morgenbesser (1980) highlight the fact that traditional agencies have often become sufficiently bureaucratized and static; therefore, new organizations are needed to meet new needs.

In our discussion we distinguish between two types of alternative organizations: those that deliver services directly to the target population, be it an individual or community, and those that are funds and foundations that raise money designed to support direct service agencies. However, all are committed to social change. These organizations differ from the traditional ones in many dimensions. We will describe these dimensions and illustrate them by using a progressive social change fund as our case study.

The Bread and Roses Community Fund was founded in 1977 as a public foundation that provides financial support to organizations that are working for social change in the greater Philadelphia area. Special priority is given to small community-based groups that have limited access to traditional funding from United Way or local foundations because they are considered too small or too controversial.

Characteristics of Alternative Organizations

The following characteristics provide a useful snapshot of alternative organizations.

(1) Commitment to Social Change

The commitment to external social change is a major stimulation in the founding of alternative organizations. Alternative organizations are not content merely to address the problem and serve the people at risk; they also feel compelled to advocate for change in the larger society.

Bread and Roses is particularly interesting in regard to its mission, which includes a commitment to social change, both internally within the organization and externally in the broader community. It does this in several ways. First, it only funds organizations that are committed to social change. Several examples of the activities of its grantee organizations serve to illustrate this commitment.

- *The Disabled in Action group is composed of people with various degrees of disability. It successfully brought to public attention the need for public transportation for people in wheelchairs and with other physical needs. This took place long before the passage of the American Disabilities Act.*
- *The Kensington Joint Action Council organized a coalition of 33 organizations in a low-income area of Philadelphia to challenge the lending policy of a major Philadelphia bank that did not meet the requirements of federal law under the Community Reinvestment Act. They won a $50 million, three-year settlement.*
- *The Philadelphia Lesbian and Gay Task Force has released a study that documents local discrimination, harassment, and violence experienced by the gay and lesbian community. It has recommended various responses, including legislation and police training.*
- *The Action Alliance of Senior Citizens of Greater Philadelphia has played a major role in the struggle to maintain special programs*

and discounts for senior citizens, including a special transit program provided by the state.

The role played by Bread and Roses on the social change dimension is only partially understood by examining the organizations it supports. It also plays a unique role itself as a watchdog in the community both at a local and state level. It encourages advocacy activity as it calls attention to problems in the community and also publicizes the activities of the organizations it supports.

(2) Internal Governance

Alternative organizations are deeply committed to social change; not only are they concerned with changing the larger external system but they are equally concerned with changing internal procedures to ensure a democratic and egalitarian operation (Schwartz, Gottesman, & Perlmutter, 1988).

The critical link between a social change mission and internal governance is empowerment. Internal change is addressed through concern with governance and participatory democracy, because decision making is a process that involves not only the traditional elites, the wealthy, but also, and especially, those who are the recipients of funding. It is the members of the latter group that are empowered as they participate in new ways.

The operating structure of Bread and Roses has been carefully designed to reflect its philosophy. It thus practices what it preaches and illustrates a successful alternative organization.

Bread and Roses is a membership organization composed of donors, volunteers, and grantee organization representatives. It is unusual in that all members meet annually to elect two boards. The board of directors is responsible for all policy and procedural decisions except for those dealing with funding. The community funding board deals with all aspects of funding, including applications, allocations, grant-making policy, and procedural decisions.

Guidelines have been developed for both boards to ensure representation by people of color, women, and sexual minorities; donors and grantees must also be represented. One staff member serves on each board, thus ensuring staff participation in policy making. A priority is to ensure a broad donor pool so that broad interests can be served. Any person who contributes $50.00 or more can serve on the board of directors, which is a critical stipulation, because more than half of the donors are wealthy. Bread and Roses has thus dealt with the problem of policy and control unduly influenced by a small cadre of wealthy donors.

(3) Special Populations

The alternative organizations are designed to meet the needs of special populations of people who are not being served by existing agencies either in the voluntary or public sectors. Usually these groups (for example, homeless people) are stigmatized by the broader society. Their values are precarious and often run counter to the secure values that underpin professional programs. The services are often exploratory, innovative, or both, and they are unavailable in the existing repertoire of the traditional agencies.

Bread and Roses defines its target populations as local advocacy organizations that, as described above, are too small, too new, or too controversial to receive traditional funding. Examples are organizations that are active in human and civil rights and workers' rights, among others.

(4) Personnel

Personnel in these organizations are either deeply committed from an ideological perspective or are themselves closely identified with, or even part of, the group at risk. Personnel consist of a broad range of people, including volunteers, paraprofessionals, and professionals. Each group is valued, and care is taken to assure that fairness and equity permeate their involvement.

(5) Organizational Size and Structure

The size and structure of these organizations are both critical variables (Silver, 1998). Smallness is valued because it permits face-to-face interaction among the participants as well as more individualized attention given to the needs of its consumers. Structure is important, as a flat hierarchy is conducive to participatory democracy, a value strongly held by these organizations.

Thus, not only is Bread and Roses itself a small operation, with only three paid staff members (an executive director, a fundraiser, and a grants associate), but the agencies it funds (that is, the grantees) are also small in size. This reflects the fact that they espouse a very specific ideology and a particular social cause that does not have a large following.

(6) Resource Base

Finally, alternative organizations are usually in a marginal position economically because the resources available to traditional social service agencies, both from public and private funds, are unavailable to them. A recent report from the *Chronicle of Philanthropy* highlights the dilemma faced by all social service agencies: "For the first time in a dozen years, contributions to the nation's largest charities declined in 2002, the result of continuing economic uncertainty among donors and heightened competition for money among charities" (Wolverton, 2003).

Given the fact that resources for the human services are generally limited, the situation is more extreme for alternative organizations. In fact, a recent study shows that only 2.4 percent of all United States institutional funding went to progressive social change philanthropy (National Network of Grantmakers, 1998). Even when supporting social change, traditional funds tend to support more mainstream, moderate activities (Jenkins, 1989). By contrast, social change funds support and encourage controversial activities among their grantees (Perlmutter & Kramer, 2001).

Consequently, in the design and development of an alternative social service agency, planning for the resource base must be a vital aspect of planning the organizational mission (Harvey & McCrohan, 1990). Bread and Roses views mission and resource development as interrelated and seeks donors from as broad an economic base as possible. Consistent with its philosophy, it values the smallest contributor and, as discussed previously, makes eligible for membership on its board anyone who donates more than $50.

Implications for Administration

The egalitarian nature of alternative social service organizations, the commitment to social change, and the other characteristics discussed above suggest that leadership and administration in these organizations is unique and must be carefully framed. This discussion will be organized around two requisites for this role: personal and organizational.

(1) Personal Requisites

The findings of a national study of social change funds clearly show that the top priorities for the alternative organization executive are the commitment to mission and the ability to articulate it to the outside world (Perlmutter & Kramer, 2001). "The executive must be committed to the mission of the organization, identified with the issues, and out in the community" (p. 43).

Consequently, of greatest importance is the individual's personal ideology and value framework, because the efforts of the organization to create changes in society are central to its existence. This emphasis requires a person who shares the commitment on a personal level; it is not enough to be a social activist in the broader sense. The particular social problem that the alternative organization is addressing should be one with which the administrator is ideologically identified. To borrow a metaphor from architecture, form follows function; that is, the mission and mandate precede organizational and structural arrangements.

The capacity for risk-taking and flexibility are also of utmost importance, because unpredictability is a reality in the growth and development of alternative organizations. What is clear is that the environment in which this takes place is not a stable one. The leader must not only be able to handle this instability, and perhaps even to thrive on the challenge, but must also set the tone that helps all personnel in the organization deal with this circumstance. The economic insecurity of the situation also creates additional stress.

The administrator in an alternative program must be comfortable with diversity, because many different types of people will be involved with the organization as consumers, supporters, funders, and volunteers. In fact, the capacity of the organization to attract people of difference is distinctly tied to its mission.

Although these personal qualifications undoubtedly limit the pool of potential candidates for administrative positions, it is important that they be recognized at the outset to prevent the personal and organizational traumas that would result from naiveté.

(2) Organizational Requisites

In understanding the organizational issues involved in the leadership of alternative organizations it is essential to point out that not only is the organization dealing with complex social problems, but this is also an organization whose mandate is typically unacceptable to the broader system. The implications of this fact of life is that the administrator must, first and foremost, serve an ongoing watchdog and advocacy function as the broader society requires continuous education and persuasion. Visibility in the community and the ability to organize and bring people together assumes a readiness and the capacity to constantly seek new audiences. In addition, the ability to deal with controversy and political situations is necessary.

While these organizations have an urgent need for continuous fundraising and development work, there is a view that this technical competence can be obtained from consultants, support centers for nonprofits, and other staff members. Given that it is impossible to find someone with all the desired qualifications, fundraising takes a second place, as leadership requires a far broader range of abilities than raising funds or grant making. A ranking of executive views of the essential leadership characteristics is as follows: ideological commitment (63%), managerial skills (58%), external communications capability (57%), fundraising skills (54%), financial (29%) and charismatic leadership (38%) skills, ability to work with volunteers (38%), and political skills (Perlmutter & Kramer, 2001).

The organization can never rest on its laurels; it must simultaneously question its programmatic approaches as well as explore new ways to meet the ever-changing circumstances and needs of its target population. Consequently, the greater the creativity and initiative, the better.

A Final Word on Administering Alternative Social Service Agencies

Alternative social service programs serve a critical function in the rapidly changing and complex society of the United States. They must be encouraged to develop, but they must also be protected and nurtured. This chapter has attempted to add to the increasing interest in this area by identifying some of their unique properties.

Leadership in this arena is complex, but there is a basic compatibility with the social work profession and their leadership preparation. The bottom line is that the administrator must carry the torch of the organization's mission, because in the alternative agency it glows like a beacon to light the way for all of its participants.

PART III

EPILOGUE:
PROFESSIONAL
ETHICS

CHAPTER 13

The Ethical Administrator

Changing Hats is intended to expose the reader to the professional, organizational, and personal dimensions of social work administration. At the same time, we have referred throughout this volume to portions of our profession's *Code of Ethics*. It is fitting that we conclude this volume with a detailed discussion of the code and its relevance for the ethical administrator.

We begin this chapter with a review of the *Code of Ethics* and then revisit all of the topics presented in this volume with an emphasis on ethical responses to the dilemmas inherent in each. A case illustration of administrative ethics follows, and the chapter concludes with some final thoughts about the ethical practice of administration in the context of the social agency.

The Ethics of Social Work Administration

Talcott Parsons (1964), in his classic discussion of the attributes of a profession, identifies ethics as a critical component for all professions. Abraham Flexner, as early as 1915, included ethics in his analysis of social work as a profession. The *Code of Ethics* was central in the development of standards for the licensure of social workers throughout the states.

The ethical precepts of the social work profession are of great importance for several reasons. First, the administrator is the head of the organization and provides leadership for the total system. As a model for others in the organization, the administrator sets the tone for the entire organization. Second, because administrators work in a pressure caldron and a highly politicized environment, they are often faced with ethical dilemmas that require resolution. It is not sufficient for administrators to simply display competence in the various domains associated with organizational leadership; rather, they "must also appreciate how each of these phenomena is fraught with ethical issues, that is, issues that raise questions about matters of right and wrong and administrators' moral duties and obligations" (Reamer, 2000, p. 69). The *Code of Ethics* provides important guidelines.

The preamble to the NASW *Code of Ethics* (1999) is a succinct statement of the purpose of the code and the role it can play.

> The primary mission of the social work profession is to enhance human well-being and help meet the basic human needs of all people, with particular attention to the needs and empowerment of people who are vulnerable, oppressed, and living in poverty. A historic and defining feature of social work is the profession's focus on individual well-being in a social context and the well-being of society. Fundamental to social work is attention to the environmental forces that create, contribute to, and address problems in living.
>
> Social workers promote social justice and social change with and on behalf of clients. "Clients" is used inclusively to refer to individuals, families, groups, organizations, and communities. Social workers are sensitive to cultural and ethnic diversity and strive to end discrimination, oppression, poverty, and other forms of social injustice. These activities may be in the form of direct practice, community organizing, supervision, consultation, administration, advocacy, social and political action, policy development and implementation, education, and research and evaluation. Social workers seek to enhance the capacity of people to address their own needs. Social workers also seek to promote

the responsiveness of organizations, communities, and other social institutions to individuals' needs and social problems.

The mission of the social work profession is rooted in a set of core values. These core values, embraced by social workers throughout the profession's history, are the foundation of social work's unique purpose and perspective:

- service
- social justice
- dignity and worth of the person
- importance of human relationships
- integrity
- competence.

This constellation of core values reflects what is unique to the social work profession. Core values, and the principles that flow from them, must be balanced within the context and complexity of the human experience. (NASW, 1999, Preamble)

Ethical Standards of the Profession

Ethical standards for the profession, first formulated as a code of ethics in the late 1950s, were revised and adopted by the NASW's 1999 Delegate Assembly. At first glance these may appear to relate more closely to clinical practice than to administrative practice. However, the following discussion will highlight the ways in which administrative practice is also informed and guided by the *Code of Ethics*. Indeed, the *Code of Ethics* underscores this point with the following statement: "These principles set forth ideals to which all social workers should aspire" (NASW, 1999, p. 3).

Social Workers' Ethical Responsibilities to Clients

The NASW *Code of Ethics* identifies an array of responsibilities in relation to clients. These include an emphasis on the primacy of the client's interests, noting issues such as ensuring client self-determination; obtaining informed consent; protecting cultural competence and social diversity; preventing conflicts of interest; ensuring privacy and confidentiality; allowing access to records; not engaging in sexual relationships or physical contact; and not allowing sexual harassment or derogatory language, among others.

These elements, while relating directly to the work of clinical practitioners, also have important implications for administrators. For example,

> The legal concept of vicarious liability imposes legal responsibility for causing an injury to someone or something that in reality had nothing whatsoever to do with actually causing the injury....When an employee is negligent on the job, the employer is legally responsible for any damage or injury the employee causes. (Claris Law, Inc., 2002, p. 1)

With this knowledge—that supervisors have a legal responsibility for the actions of their supervisees—it is evident that administrators must be aware of their supervisees' behaviors when interacting with their clients. Moreover, administrators have an obligation to develop policies that ensure clients' rights and must provide training for direct practitioners to promote ethical behaviors. The primacy of adhering to legal obligations for reporting client abuse reflects recognition of the vulnerability of clients.

Social Workers' Ethical Responsibilities to Colleagues

The elements of this standard address the social workers' professional comportment with colleagues and focuses on a broad array of behaviors. These include respecting confidentiality; promoting interdisciplinary collaboration; resolving disputes involving colleagues; providing consultation; cooperating in referrals for services; and not engaging in sexual relationships, sexual harassment, or other unethical conduct.

In upholding these ethical standards, administrators should be aware of applicable laws and their own legal obligations with regard to the behaviors of their colleagues. When unethical activities of colleagues are known to the administrator, he or she must report them to either upper administration or legal authorities.

Social Workers' Ethical Responsibilities in Practice Settings

This section of the NASW *Code of Ethics* emphasizes the responsibility to the agency as the basis for professional practice and is concerned with providing effective supervision and consultation, education and training, and performance evaluations. It also includes carrying the responsibility for maintaining client records, the administration of agency finances, and maintaining positive labor–management relations.

The principle appears, on the surface, to apply primarily to administrators, but it also addresses client and staff well-being as essential elements in the agency setting. Administrators serve as role models for their supervisees, and in that capacity they must always exemplify ethical behavior. We can also point to implications for clients when considering ethical obligations in practice settings, for if direct care workers are not effectively supervised, evaluated, and trained, clients will suffer.

Social Workers' Ethical Responsibilities as Professionals

The NASW *Code of Ethics* is concerned with the integrity of the profession and its values, ethics, knowledge, and mission. This fourth principle in the *Code of Ethics* addresses a variety of professional concerns. The administrator is responsible not only for ensuring that the staff members are ethical in their performance but also for preventing the unauthorized and unqualified practice of social work through careful hiring practices.

Professional conduct is important for all social workers but is perhaps more so for administrators. Administrators are expected to understand the external laws that govern practice and to develop internal policies that are humane yet exacting in their expectations for ethical work performance. Illegal activities of any kind are expressly prohibited, and administrators have an obligation to ensure not only that clients are not harmed by illegal activities, but also that the resources of the organization are not misused.

The administrator is in a position to ensure that agency services are accurately represented in all the public relations material prepared for dissemination. Not only must the administrator be concerned with access to and availability of the services of his or her agency, but he or she should also be active in advocating for social policy related to the agency's target populations.

Social Workers' Ethical Responsibilities to the Social Work Profession

The *Code of Ethics* addresses the broader aspects of the profession with a focus on the integrity of the profession, evaluation, and research. Contributing to the social work knowledge base through research provides a critical path that leads to deeper understanding about the needs of target populations, effective services, and, perhaps most important, ineffective services.

The increasing emphasis on technology transfer underscores the need for communication between social work researchers and practitioners. This takes place in a two-way relationship: researchers must inform practitioners what they learn about practice effectiveness, and practitioners (both clinical and administrative) must share information about changing needs or characteristics of their target populations as well as promising practices that can be employed by other social workers.

Social Workers' Ethical Responsibilities to the Broader Society

The final principle of the NASW *Code of Ethics* focuses on the general well-being and needs of society. Attention is paid to public participation, dealing with public emergencies, and participating in social and political action.

Although all social workers share in this obligation, administrators are in a unique position in this regard. It is crucial that administrators accept the role of advocate when they observe changes in the agency's client profile, when needs in common are expressed by many clients, or if policies are promulgated or being considered that might impede the service delivery process. These activities relate not only to the specific agency in which they work but also reflect the administrator's responsibilities to broader social welfare concerns.

Applying the *Code of Ethics* to This Volume

Having visited our profession's *Code of Ethics* while wearing the administrator's hat, we close this volume with a review each of the previous chapters as they relate to this code.

The Context of Social Work Administration

If one accepts the proposition that social work agencies operate in a turbulent environment, then it follows that the administrator has the responsibility to be a proactive leader; while doing nothing is also an active choice, it is incompatible with the code of ethics. However, each option is fraught with ethical implications.

Let us start with a situation where an administrator observes that funding or policy changes in the external environment can be expected to have an effect on the agency's ability to continue its service mission. If that administrator chooses to do nothing, it is possible that fiscal and policy support for the agency's services will wane or disappear. In that event, the clients who depended upon the agency will not find relief for the problems that brought them to the agency in the first place. This may result in continued addiction, violence, trauma, or poverty in their lives.

Alternatively, the administrator who is proactive but who has not carefully thought through a strategy in the context of the agency's mission may make the mistake of supplanting the goal of client benefit in favor of that of agency survival. This is especially true when for-profit organizational forms are selected that require the ascendance of the motive for profit over that of client needs.

The ethical administrator, when faced with these dilemmas, must use integrity in the role of proactive leader to identify solutions that protect both the agency and its target population while working in concert with staff members, clients, and board members. Effective strategies may include legislative advocacy, identification of alternative funding sources, and strategic short- and long-range planning.

Making the Shift from Practice to Administration

It is important to consider the ethical implications of using the opportunity to shift from practitioner to administrator. If one considers this an opportunity to influence better collegial relationships and better agency practice, this indeed follows the ethical precepts of our profession. However, if the shift is done to access power for personal gain and privilege only, this violates ethical professional behavior.

Personal concerns might also impede the social worker's movement from practice to administration, such as concerns about changed peer relationships, discomfort with power or authority, lack of self-confidence, or burnout. In each of these situations, competencies that the worker might successfully apply to the managerial role will be lost as a resource for the agency. The *Code of Ethics* requires the setting aside of personal agendas in favor of collective needs, be they in the agency or in the broader society.

The Dilemmas of Middle Management

The role of the middle manager described in Chapter 4 presents challenges as well as opportunities. Challenges typically arise from conflicting demands placed upon the middle manager from upper administration and subordinates. The ethical considerations inherent in this context arise from the middle manager's response to these conflicts.

The ethical middle manager makes decisions from a stance of organizational and client benefit. When subordinates are unhappy in their jobs, burned out, disdainful of organizational policies and procedures, or disrespectful, it is the responsibility of the middle manager to deal with these behaviors directly. If there is no change, the middle manager may find it necessary to communicate these behaviors to upper administration. While the consequences may be that individuals are terminated, that the manager is perceived as unable to effectively supervise subordinates, or that subordinates perceive the manager as an informer, to withhold this information because of fear of reprisal is unethical. It is equally unethical to fail to act when clients do not receive high-quality services because of dissension among subordinates.

In a similar vein, middle managers often receive directives from upper administration that require implementation by their supervisees of policies and procedures with which they do not agree. To ignore, sabotage, or otherwise undermine the intent of these directives constitutes unethical managerial practice. However, at the same time the middle manager should work to change a poor policy or procedure and to influence upper-level deliberations. Providing information about the needs of clients, subordinates, or program services to administrators who are deliberating changes in policies or procedures is an important contribution.

In short, the middle manager is, by definition, caught between two worlds: upper administration and subordinates. The ethical middle manager will facilitate communication between these two groups to ensure that services are enhanced and that the integrity of all concerned is upheld.

Administrative Advocacy and the Management of Change

The role of the administrator related to administrative advocacy is central to the social work core value of social justice. Social justice is a goal in relation to the agency both on the outside and inside. External to the agency, advocacy serves to educate the public as well as policymakers about the needs of the client population. Internal to the agency, social justice is expressed by means of the management of change that is designed to improve the delivery of services. Ethical dilemmas are inherent in each.

The ethical administrator who seeks social justice in the broader community has the opportunity to provide information about the target population that can elicit a sympathetic view of the situation. The

New York Times approach of reporting the 100 neediest cases is a good example of this opportunity, and administrators can take the opportunity to provide the information needed by the *Times* in the form of data or client stories. The emphasis should be on the negative effects of the status quo on clients, such as inadequate funding or service availability, system fragmentation, and limited opportunities for empowerment.

Also, when multiple strategies are available to the administrator for implementing advocacy efforts, the ethical administrator will select those that offer the highest benefit for the least cost. For example, consensus building is a change strategy that has low risk but that may result in little or no change; alternatively, conflict strategies may result in dramatic changes in the status quo, but public perception of the organization may shift to the negative. The social work administrator must make a judgment as to which path to follow.

Internally, administrators express their roles as change agent by undertaking organizational change from a position of inclusion and deliberation, compatible with the *Code of Ethics* position on the social worker's ethical responsibility to colleagues. To impose change on subordinates or clients without gaining their input can lead to failure of the change effort. The end result of these missed opportunities is that internal change is ignored or undermined and the intended client or organizational benefit will not be achieved. Moreover, a climate of apprehension will be established whereby future change efforts will be suspect.

At the same time, in developing a strategy for internal change the ethical administrator must proceed from a vantage point of social interest whereby it is clearly communicated that the advocacy effort is intended to improve the lot of clients, workers, services, and the larger society. In short, change for the sake of change or to serve self-aggrandizement is unethical.

The Administrator's Role in Agency Governance

Our discussion of the administrator's role in agency governance emphasizes the importance of the relationship between the administrator and the board of directors. This relationship forms the basis for our discussion for ethical practice in this dimension.

The board of directors relies heavily for its policy making and planning roles upon the administrator for information regarding agency, client, and staff needs. The ethical administrator will provide comprehensive information based on an open and honest assessment of the internal as well as external environment with an emphasis on changes that are needed to improve services. It is unethical as well as inappropriate to provide partial information or misinformation that will sway the discussion. It is equally unethical for the administrator to appear to support the policies developed by the board of directors, only to undermine their implementation.

In regard to board member selection, while the board is responsible for the process of voting in its members, nominees are suggested with significant input from the agency's administrator. The ethical administrator will ensure that the board is composed of individuals who will use their skills and resources to improve the agency's ability to provide services to its target population and, when appropriate, to challenge the status quo, both internally and externally. The risk of unethical practice is found in attempts of the administrator to influence the selection of board members based on their perceived ability to support, without question, his or her initiatives.

The Administrator as Politician

The proactive management of change requires the ethical administrator to evaluate external threats to the agency and its client population and to implement appropriate political strategies designed to reduce those threats. Political behavior is implicit in this process.

For example, a tenuous relationship may exist between social agency administrators and public policymakers; each may have misconceptions about the other. Social work administrators may be seen as primarily seeking resources for the survival of their agencies, with the goal of client benefit perceived as secondary, whereas politicians may be viewed as serving their own political agendas for power and re-election. It is the responsibility of the administrator to seek to reduce this tension by undertaking political strategies designed to change these perceptions and to improve the position of the agency. The aim is the forging of effective relationships in accordance with the *Code of Ethics* and its focus on the profession's responsibility to society.

The Administrator and Interorganizational Relations

Our position concerning the importance of interorganizational relationships raises some interesting and complex ethical concerns. In a time of shrinking resources, many agencies feel threatened and turn inward, unready to risk collaboration which they fear may take away potential resources (for example, money or clients).

The *Code of Ethics* suggests that a focus on the primacy of meeting client needs requires that the administrator creatively seek collaborations that would serve the clients most effectively while protecting the agency's well-being. Thus, if an agency has resources that it can offer to other organizations to increase the breadth and scope of services available to those in the community with common needs, a refusal to consider a strategic alliance may be unethical. At the same time, a strategy of alliance for the sake of achieving dominance over other agencies in the service sector is equally unethical (for example, some administrators value size as a determinant of organizational effectiveness).

Thus, it is critical that the ethical administrator carefully weigh the benefits and costs as well as the underlying rationale when considering strategic alliances, and the overarching goal should always be meeting the agency's mission as related to client benefit.

The Administrator's Use of Communication

Effective communication within a social service organization is an essential aspect of the administrator's role. It can serve to unite or divide staff members, who ideally should be working together toward the common goal of supporting the agency's mission.

Examples of unethical communication practices are the following:

- discussing personal life situations, such as illness or divorce, of one staff member with others

- telling an employee that her work is satisfactory and then preparing a negative performance appraisal
- neglecting to ensure that client confidentiality is upheld
- complaining about upper-administration directives to subordinates
- arbitrarily establishing competition among work units or individual workers
- publicly discussing workers' inability to do their jobs well
- inviting workers' input on decisions that have already been made.

In all of these examples the unethical administrator diminishes her or his standing by establishing an environment of mistrust. To maintain the integrity of the agency, ethical communication must serve the purpose of fostering openness, information sharing, and trust, all hallmarks of professionalism.

The Administrator's Work with Volunteers

Key decisions regarding appropriate roles for volunteers within service organizations should be based on the potential contribution of those volunteers to the agency's mission. This is of ethical concern, given that agencies under fiscal duress are tempted to use volunteers in the provision of services. It is inappropriate to appoint volunteers to jobs that require professional training or certification and which should be filled by professionals. Among the many determinants of this consideration are client confidentiality and safety. If either is jeopardized by the use of volunteers in professional roles, then it is unethical to initiate or continue their use. It would be equally unethical to assign untrained volunteers to clients who might present physical or psychological danger to the volunteers.

Obtaining and Administering Financial Resources

Fiduciary responsibility is uppermost among the obligations of the social administrator, and it is essential for organizational legitimacy and survival. The ethical considerations of this role center on the use of financial resources for their intended purposes, clearly spelled out in the *Code of Ethics* discussion of the responsibility to the employing organization.

The application of external funding for its intended purpose is a contractual responsibility. Unethical practices in this regard vary from the subtle to the illegal and may include, for example, the assignment of funding intended for one program unit to another, the falsification of fiscal reports, or the use of nonadministrative funds for travel or supplies. The most dramatic example of this unfolded in the 1990s, when William Aramony, Executive Director of United Way, was convicted of fraud for his misuse of the organization's funds.

Administering Alternative Social Service Agencies

Alternative organizations are committed to meeting the needs of marginalized populations. They have a special mission, usually focused on one particular target population. The ethical administrator must work to ensure that the mission of the alternative organization is not distorted by the availability of funds for other pressing target populations and community needs for which funding is available. Similarly, the involvement of an array of people in the decision-making process is an essential component that must be protected (Perlmutter & Kramer, 2001).

A Case Study

The complexity of adhering to the code of ethics is effectively illustrated by the experience of Oceanview, a nonprofit agency that receives its funding from a state Department of Public Welfare. This case touches many elements of the NASW *Code of Ethics* discussed above.

Oceanview provides transitional living arrangements for mentally retarded adults. The agency seeks to develop in its clients those skills, behaviors, and attitudes essential to independent living. The service is organized through individualized programming and through attempts to integrate clients into the community.

The staff members are critical in providing the agency's services, because they create a less restrictive environment with an emphasis on experiences that enhance an individual's ability to succeed. The staff members are not highly educated, however, and the agency depends primarily on on-the-job training. The work is stressful, the wages are low, and the turnover rate is high.

The administration of Oceanview was struggling with the implementation of a drug-testing policy for all of its staff. There were a few cases in which staff used drugs, and there also were rumors of drug selling by the staff on Oceanview's premises. It was believed that only a small minority of direct care staff were involved. The administration struggled with the question of whether it was ethical to invade each employee's privacy by testing for drugs across the board when the majority of staff were clean.

When the rumor spread throughout the agency that drug testing might take place, the staff became outraged. It is believed that no issue in the agency's history ever created so intense a response. The staff felt that their employer should not regulate what they did on their own time. In addition, many employees did not think it was ethical to test everyone because a few persons may have been using drugs. Some felt drug use was no worse than drinking a beer.

Some of the employees who admitted to smoking marijuana on days off were some of Oceanview's best. Many threatened to quit if the policy was put into effect. This put the administration in a tough position, because the administrator believed that the safety of the clients was the central issue. If staff were working under the influence of drugs, clients were not being given the best care possible and may have been in danger. The administration faced a dilemma: If the agency submitted its staff to drug testing, some might leave at a time when the turnover rate of direct care staff was at an all-time high.

However, the majority of the administrative staff believed that the advantages of drug testing outweighed the disadvantages. Their view was that the agency had been lucky to that point but that if drug testing was not instituted, a real disaster was imminent. Client lives cannot be put at risk. Drugs, including marijuana, are illegal, and their use by the staff who work at Oceanview could not be tolerated.

There were no simple answers. The administrator of Overview decided to handle the situation in a participatory manner.

Oceanview has a forum known as "Task Force" in which staff can come and discuss any issues they believe are important. The administration decided to use this as a vehicle both to inform employees and to explore the possible benefits to the agency of a drug-testing policy. Oceanview made clear to its employees that their input was wanted and that drug testing would not be implemented without first trying to come up with alternatives that would produce a drug-free environment.

Task Force provided a mechanism to introduce an issue that was very controversial. Because drugs had an effect on the safety and well-being of everyone at the agency, the issue was raised at the first meeting as being not only an administrative concern but also a concern of the direct care staff. The attendance at this meeting was the highest of any that had been held. The administration could see that the staff were very concerned with this highly volatile subject. The staff respected the fact that the administration did not institute a drug-testing policy without first having a forum with the staff. The staff felt their input really made a difference.

Some staff members actually admitted that after listening to the administrative reasons for developing a drug-testing policy they felt that it was in the best interests of those being served and that drug use should be prohibited. The staff agreed that if an alternative that would reap the same results as drug testing could not be developed, they would give up their rights to privacy to ensure the best possible care for those being served.

It is clear that there was no easy answer to this situation or to other complex ones. The NASW *Code of Ethics*, however, can provide an important guide to the decision-making process. As Reamer (2000) points out,

> Administrators face a never-ending series of complex duties. Their ethical responsibilities—which necessarily involve decisions about moral duty and obligation—constitute the core of their professional mission. Administrators' task is to cultivate both the internal and external controls and compass that are essential for ethical practice. (p. 83)

The Final Word

We return to the core values expressed in our profession's *Code of Ethics* for guidance as we close this volume: "service; social justice; dignity and worth of the person; importance or human relationships; integrity; and competence" (NASW, 1999, p. 1). These core values permeate the role and performance of administrators. They underscore the importance of ethical practice and the fact that the management of change, whether personal, professional, or organizational, must be accomplished with careful attention to the core values and ethics of the profession.

After several years of experience in the field, practitioners often have the opportunity to move into administration. The incentives are usually great in terms of both salary and status. These incentives, although seductive, are misleading, because they skirt the real issues that should be dealt with in making this shift. The bottom line is whether the nature of the work of the administrator is appealing and challenges the individual to try a new, but related, professional route.

Given the demands on administrators and the complexity of administration in social service, it is essential that the motivation be based on personal interests, preferences, and capabilities. Equal status and recognition should be awarded to the advanced practitioner who is providing the best possible service to consumers of social service, and the decision should be based on an understanding of both the clinical and administrative roles as well as an understanding of oneself in relation to those roles. This is not a simple choice, especially because most social workers enter the profession to become involved in direct service, be it with individual clients, groups, or communities. Changing hats entails some rather fundamental new learning and behavior.

It is assumed that the inclination to make the transition to administration does exist and that those individuals who are thinking about making the transition are seeking both a change and a challenge in professional life. Although there are various ways to achieve professional satisfaction, many of which are appropriate, relevant, and important, the purpose of this volume has been to focus on social work administration as a career.

Four basic assumptions presented in Chapter 1 serve as the underpinnings for the practice of social work administration. First, the route to social work administration is best traveled from the starting point of direct practice experience. Second, the social work administrator must be proactive, with a vision of the future that serves to impel the organization forward to better meet clients' needs. Third, the social work administrator must serve as an advocate for the constituency being served and educate the broader, external community about special client interests and needs. Fourth, the social work administrator must be constantly seeking to empower both the staff members and the clients of the agency.

Finally, the point was made that these four assumptions may, in fact, be critical in distinguishing the field of social work administration from other forms of management. Identification of these unique attributes is a fruitful quest if it serves to sharpen performance. If the reader finds these assumptions compatible with the notion of an effective administrator, and if the reader is challenged to try them on for size, it is probably time to take the importance first step in determining a career move.

References

2-1-1 Big Bend. (2003). *Volunteer Reflections*. Retrieved from http://www.211bigbend.org/volunteer/reflections.htm. on January 12, 2004.

Ad Hoc Committee on Advocacy (1969). The social worker as advocate: Champion of social victims. *Social Work, 14,* 16–22.

Adams, C. T., & Perlmutter, F. D. (1991). Commercial venturing and the transformation of America's voluntary social welfare agencies. *Nonprofit and Voluntary Sector Quarterly, 20,* 25–38.

Aronson, R. L. (1985). Unionism among professional employees in the private sector. *Industrial and Labor Relations Review,* 6(2), 141–56.

Association for Volunteer Administration (1999). *Portrait of a profession: Volunteer administration.* Richmond, VA: Association for Volunteer Administration.

Austin, D. M. (2000). Social work and social welfare administration: A historical perspective. In R. J. Patti (Ed.), *The handbook of social welfare management* (pp. 27–54). Thousand Oaks, CA: Sage.

Bargal, D. (2000). The manager as leader. In R. J. Patti (Ed.), *The handbook of social welfare management* (pp. 303–320). Thousand Oaks, CA: Sage.

Brager, G., & Holloway, S. (1978). *Changing human service organizations.* New York: The Free Press.

Braithwaite, C. (1938). *The voluntary citizen.* London: Methuen.

Brody, R. (2000). *Effectively managing human service organizations.* Thousand Oaks, CA: Sage.

Campus Compact (2000). *Highlights and trends in student service and service learning: Statistics from the 1999 member and faculty survey.* Providence, RI: Campus Compact.

Chernesky, R. H. (1998). Advancing women in the managerial ranks. In R. L. Edwards, J. A. Yankey, & M. A. Altpeter (Eds.), *Skills for effective management of nonprofit organizations* (pp. 200–218). Washington, DC: NASW Press.

Claris Law, Inc. (2002). Vicarious liability . Retrieved from http://www.injuryboard.com/tort13.cfm on January 12, 2004

Cnaan, R. A., with Boddie, S. C., Handy, F., Yancey, G., & Schneider, R. (2002). *The invisible caring hand: American congregations and the provision of welfare.* New York: New York University Press.

Cnaan, R. A., & Boddie, S. C. (2002). Charitable choice and faith-based welfare: A call for social work. *Social Work, 47,* 247–235.

Coalition Letter (2002). Coalition letter supporting increased access to education and training for TANF recipients . Retrieved from http://www.naswdc.org on January 12, 2004.

Council on Social Work Education (2002). Education policy and accreditation standards . Retrieved from http://www.cswe.org on January 12, 2004.

De Shazer, S. (1991). *Keys to solution in brief therapy.* New York: W. W. Norton.

DeSchweinitz, K. (1943). *England's road to social security.* Philadelphia: University of Pennsylvania Press.

Eadie, D. C. (1999). Building the capacity to lead innovation. In R. L. Edwards, J. A. Yankey, & M. A. Altpeter (Eds.), *Skills for effective management of nonprofit organizations* (pp. 27–44). Washington, DC: NASW Press.

Edwards, R. L., Yankey, J. A., & Altpeter, M. A. (1998). Managing effectively in an environment of competing values. In R. L. Edwards, J. A. Yankey, & M. A. Altpeter (Eds.), *Skills for effective management of nonprofit organizations* (pp. 5–24). Washington, DC: NASW Press.

Ellis, S. J., & Noyes, K. H. (1976). *By the people: A history of Americans as volunteers.* Philadelphia: Energize.

Emery, F. E., & Trist, E. L. (1969). The causal texture of organizational environments. In F. E. Emery (Ed.), *Systems thinking* (pp. 241–257). New York: Penguin Books.

Epstein, L., & Brown, L. B. (2002). *Brief treatment and a new look at the task-centered approach.* Boston: Allyn and Bacon.

Ezell, M. (2001). *Advocacy in the human services.* Belmont, CA: Wadsworth.

Ezell, M. (2000). Financial management. In R. J. Patti (Ed.), *The handbook of social welfare management* (pp. 377–394). Thousand Oaks, CA: Sage.

Family Service of America (1960). *Considerations involved in the use of public funds by family agencies.* New York: Family Service of America.

Finch, W. A., Jr. (1982). Declining public social service resources: A managerial problem. *Administration in Social Work, 6,* 19–28.

References

Gallos, J. V., Ramsey, V. J., & Associates. (1997). *Teaching diversity: Listening to the soul, speaking from the heart.* San Francisco: Jossey-Bass.

Gardner, J. W. (1990). *On leadership.* New York: The Free Press.

Gibelman, M. (2000). Structural and fiscal characteristics of social service agencies. In R. J. Patti (Ed.), *The handbook of social welfare management* (pp. 113–132). Thousand Oaks, CA: Sage.

Gibelman, M. (2003). *Navigating human service organizations.* Chicago: Lyceum.

Gibelman, M., & Kraft, S. (1996). Advocacy as a core agency program: Planning considerations for voluntary human service agencies. *Administration in Social Work, 20*(4), 43–59.

Gibelman, M., & Schervish, P. H. (1997). *Who we are: A second look.* Washington, DC: NASW Press.

Golan, N. (1978). *Treatment in crisis situations.* New York: The Free Press.

Gomory, T. (2001). A fallibilistic response to Thyer's theory of theory-free empirical research in social work practice. *Journal of Social Work Education, 37*(1), 26–50.

Gray, M. J., Ondaatje, E. H., Fricker, R., Geschwind, S., Goldman, C. A., Kaganoff, T., Robyn, A., Sundt, M., Vogelgesang, L., & Klein, S. P. (1998). *Coupling service and learning in higher education: The final report of the evaluation of the Learn and Serve America, Higher Education Program.* Washington, DC: RAND Corporation.

Grossman, B. & Morgenbesser, M. (1980). Alernative social service settings: Opportunities for social work education. *Journal of Humanities, 8,* 59–76.

Guardian Ad Litem (2002). *State of Florida Fifth Judicial Circuit Guardian Ad Litem Program: Our mission.* Retrieved from http://www.guardian adlitem.org/about.htm#mission on January 12, 2004.

Gummer, B. (1979). Is the social worker in public welfare an endangered species? *Public Welfare, 57*(Fall), 12–21.

Gummer, B. (1980). Organization theory. In F. D. Perlmutter & S. Slavin (Eds.), *Leadership in social administration* (pp. 22–49). Philadelphia: Temple University Press.

Gummer, B. (1990). *The politics of social administration: Managing organizational politics in social agencies.* Englewood Cliffs, NJ: Prentice Hall.

Gummer, B. (1998). Current perspectives on diversity in the workforce: How diverse is diverse? *Administration in Social Work, 22*(1), 85–100.

Handy, C. (1994). *The age of paradox.* Boston: Harvard Business School Press.

Harvey, J. W., & McCrohan, K. F. (1990). Changing conditions for fund raising and philanthropy. In J. Van Til (Ed.), *Critical issues in American philanthropy* (pp. 222–241). San Francisco: Jossey-Bass.

Hasenfeld, Y. (1983). *Human service organizations.* Englewood Cliffs, NJ: Prentice Hall.

Hasenfeld, Y. (2000). Social welfare administration and organizational theory. In R. J. Patti (Ed.), *The handbook of social welfare management* (pp. 89–112). Thousand Oaks, CA: Sage.

Haveman, H. A. (1992). Between a rock and a hard place: Organizational change and performance under conditions of fundamental environmental information. *Administrative Science Quarterly, 37,* 68–75.

Hawkins, F., & Gunther, J. (1998). Managing for quality. In R. L. Edwards, J. A. Yankey, & M. A. Altpeter (Eds.), *Skills for effective management of nonprofit organizations.* Washington, DC: NASW Press.

Haynes, K. S., & Mickelson, J. S. (2000). *Affecting change: Social workers in the political arena* (4th ed.). New York: Longman.

Henning, M., & Jardim, A. (1977). *The managerial woman.* New York: Anchor Press/Doubleday.

Holland, T. P. (1999). Strengthening board performance. In R. L. Edwards, J. A. Yankey, & M. A. Altpeter (Eds.), *Skills for effective management of nonprofit organizations* (pp. 425–452). Washington, DC: NASW Press.

Iglehart, A. P. (2000). Managing for diversity and empowerment in social services. In R. J. Patti (Ed.), *The handbook of social welfare management* (pp. 425–443). Thousand Oaks, CA: Sage.

Jenkins, J. C. (1989). Social movement philanthropy and American democracy. In R. Magat (Ed.), *Philanthropic giving: Studies in varieties and goals* (pp. 292–314). New York: Oxford University Press.

Kettner, P. M. (2002). *Achieving excellence in the management of human service organizations.* Boston: Allyn & Bacon.

Kettner, P., Daley, J. M., & Nichols, A. W. (1985). *Initiating change in organizations and communities: A macro practice model.* Monterey, CA: Brooks/Cole.

Kirst-Ashman, K. K., & Gull, G. H. (1997). *Generalist practice with organizations and communities.* Chicago: Nelson-Hall.

Koeske, G. F., & Koeske, R. (2000). The individual in the organization: The impact of human service workers' attributes on job response. In R. J. Patti (Ed.), *The handbook of social welfare management* (pp. 219–241). Thousand Oaks, CA: Sage.

Lee, P. R. (1937). *Social work as cause and function.* New York: Columbia University Press.

Levy, C. (1979). The ethics of management. *Administration in Social Work, 3*(3), 277–288.

Lewis, J. A., Lewis, M. D., & Souflée, F. (1991). *Management of human service organizations* (2nd ed.). Belmont, CA: Brooks/Cole.

Lewis, S., & Crook, W. P. (2001). Shifting sands: An AIDS service organization adapts to a changing environment. *Administration in Social Work, 25*(2), 1–20.

Lindblad-Goldberg, M., Dore, M., & Stern, L. (1998). *Creating competence from chaos: A comprehensive guide to home-based services.* New York: W. W. Norton.

Lohman, R. A. (1984). Resource development as executive leadership. In F. D. Perlmutter (Ed.), *Human services at risk* (pp. 93–109). Lexington, MA: Lexington Books.

Marris, P., & Rein, M. (1967). *Dilemmas of social reform.* New York: Atherton.

Manser, G., & Cass, R. H. (1976). *Volunteerism at the crossroads.* New York: Family Service of America.

Martin, L. L. (1993). *Total quality management in human service organizations.* Newbury Park, CA: Sage.

Martin, L. L. (2001). *Financial management for human service administrators.* Needham Heights, MA: Allyn & Bacon

Martin, L. L. (2000). The environmental context of social welfare administration. In R. J. Patti (Ed.), *The handbook of social welfare management* (pp. 55–67). Thousand Oaks, CA: Sage.

Maslow, A. H. (1976). Management as a psychological experiment. In W. E. Nord (Ed.), *Concepts and controversy in organizational behavior* (2nd ed.). Pacific Palisades, CA: Goodyear Publishing.

McNamara, C. (1999). *Basic definition of organization. Management assistance program for nonprofits.* Retrieved from http://www.mapnp.org/library/org_thry/org_defn.htm on January 12, 2004.

Menefee, D. (2000). What managers do and why they do it. In R. J. Patti (Ed.), *The handbook of social welfare management* (pp. 247–266). Thousand Oaks, CA: Sage.

Meyter, H. J., Borgatta, E. F. & Jones, W. C. 1965. *Girls at vocational high: an experiment in social work intervention.* New York: Russell Sage Foundation.

Millett, K. (1974). *Flying.* St. Albans, England: Granada.

Minuchin, S. (1974). *Families and family therapy.* Cambridge, MA: Harvard University Press.

National Association of Social Workers (1999). *Code of ethics.* Retrieved from http://www.naswdc.org/pubs/code/ on January 12, 2004.

National Association of Social Workers (2003). Social work profession. Retrieved from https://www.socialworkers.org/pressroom/features/general/profession.asp on January 12, 2004.

National Network of Grantmakers (1998). Social change grantmaking in the U.S. *Research Report.* Retrieved from http://www.ng.org/ourprograms/research/socchangeppr.htm on January 12, 2004.

Naylor, H. H. (1976). *Leadership for volunteering.* New York: Dryden.

Netting, F. E., Kettner, P. M., & McMurtry, S. L. (1998). *Social work macro practice* (2nd ed.). New York: Longman.

Neugeboren, B. (1991). *Organization, policy and practice in the human services.* New York: Longman.

Ostrander, S. A. (1989). Private social services: Obstacles to the welfare state? *Nonprofit and Voluntary Sector Quarterly, 18*(1), 24–45.

Parsons, T. (1961). An outline of the social system. In T. Parsons, E. Shills, K. D. Naegle, & J. R. Pitts (Eds.), *Theories of society* (pp. 38–39). New York: The Free Press.

Parsons, T. (1964). The professions and social structure. In *Essays of sociological theory.* New York: Free Press.

Patti, R., & Resnick, H. (1985). Leadership and change in child welfare organizations. In H. Laird & C. Hartman (Eds.), *Handbook of child welfare* (pp. 269–288). Glencoe, IL: The Free Press.

Perlmutter, F. D. (1971). Public funds and private agencies. *Child Welfare, 50,* 264–270.

———. (1980). The executive bind: Constraints upon leadership. In F. D. Perlmutter & S. Slavin (Eds.), *Leadership in social administration* (pp. 53–71). Philadelphia: Temple University Press.

Perlmutter, F. D. (1982). The professionalization of volunteer administration. *Journal of Voluntary Action Research, 11,* 97–107.

Perlmutter, F. D. (1983). Caught in between: The middle management bind. *Administration in Social Work, 8*(2), 147–161.

Perlmutter, F. D. (1984). The professionalization of volunteer administration. In F. G. Schwartz (Ed.), *Voluntarism and social work practice.* Lanham, MD: University Press of America.

Perlmutter, F. D., & Dunham, D. (1965). Using teenagers to supplement casework services. *Social Work, 19,* 41–46.

Perlmutter, F. D., & Adams, C. T. (1990). The voluntary sector and for profit ventures: the transformation of American social welfare. *Administration in Social Work, 14*(1), 1–14.

Perlmutter, F. D., & Adams, C. T. (1994). Family service executives in a hostile environment. *The Journal of Contemporary Human Services, 75*(7), 439–446.

Perlmutter, F. D., & Cnaan, R. A. (1993). Challenging human service organizations to redefine volunteer roles. *Administration in Social Work*, 17(4),77–95.

Perlmutter, F. D., Bailey, D., & Netting, F. E. (2001). *Managing human resources in the human services: Supervisory challenges.* New York: Oxford University Press.

Perlmutter, F. D., & Gummer, B. (1995). Managing organizational transformation. In R. Herman and Associates (Eds.), *The Jossey-Bass handbook of nonprofit leadership and management* (pp. 227–246). San Francisco: Jossey-Bass.

Perlmutter, F. D., & Kramer, V. (2001). *Social change funds: Strategies for survival.* A working paper of the nonprofit sector research fund. Washington, DC: The Aspen Institute.

Pfeffer, J. (1992). Understanding power in organizations. *California Management Review, 34,* 20–50.

Phillips, M. C. (1984). Motivation and expectation in successful volunteerism. In F. C. Schwartz (Ed.), *Voluntarism and social work practice: A growing collaboration* (pp. 139–146). Lanham, MD: University Press of America.

Powell, W. W., & Friedken, R. (1987). Organizational change in nonprofit organizations. In W.W. Powell (Ed.), *The nonprofit sector: A research handbook* (pp. 180–192). New Haven, CT: Yale University Press.

Randall, R. (1979). Presidential power and bureaucratic intransigence: The influence of the Nixon administration on welfare policy. *American Political Science Review, 73,* 795–810.

Rapoport, L. (1970). Crisis intervention as a mode of brief treatment. In R. W. Roberts & R. H. Nee (Eds .), *Theories of social casework* (pp. 267–311). Chicago: University of Chicago Press.

Rapp, C. A., & Poertner, J. (1992). *Social administration: A client-centered approach.* White Plains, NY: Longman.

Reamer, F. G. (2000). Administrative ethics. In R. J. Patti (Ed.), *The handbook of social welfare management* (pp. 69–86). Thousand Oaks, CA: Sage.

Richmond, M. E. (1917). *Social diagnosis.* New York: Russell Sage Foundation.

Robinson, G., & Barnett, L. (1996). *Service learning and community colleges: Where we are.* Washington, DC: American Association of Community Colleges.

Routh, T. A. (1977). *The volunteer and community agencies.* Springfield, IL: Charles C. Thomas.

Schindler-Rainman, E., & Lippett, R. (1977). *The volunteer community.* LaJolla, CA: University Associates.

Schmid, H. (2000). Agency-environment relations: Understanding task environments. In R. J. Patti (Ed.), *The handbook of social welfare management* (pp. 133–154). Thousand Oaks, CA: Sage.

Schneider, R. L., & Lester, L. (2001). *A new framework for action: Social work advocacy*. Belmont, CA: Wadsworth.

Schoech, D. (2000). Managing information for decision making. In R. J. Patti (Ed.), *The handbook of social welfare management* (pp. 321–360). Thousand Oaks, CA: Sage.

Schwartz, A. Y., Gottesman, E. W., & Perlmutter, F. D. (1988). Blackwell: A case study in feminist administration. In F. D. Perlmutter (Ed.), *Alternative social agencies: administrative strategies* (pp. 5–15). New York: Haworth Press.

Selig, M. K., et al. (1963). The challenge of public funds to private agencies. *Journal of Jewish Communal Service, 39,* 368–377.

Selznick, P. (1957). *Leadership in administration.* New York: Harper & Row.

Shera, W., & Page, J. (1995). Creating more effective human service organizations through strategies of empowerment. *Administration in Social Work, 19,* 1–15.

Silver, I. (1998). Buying an activist identity: Reproducing class through social movement philanthropy. *Sociological Perspectives, 41,* 303–321.

Slavin, S. (1980). A theoretical framework for social administration. In F. D. Perlmutter & S. Slavin (Eds.), *Leadership in social administration* (pp. 3–21). Philadelphia: Temple University Press.

Stern, M. (1984). The politics of American social welfare. In F. D. Perlmutter (Ed.), *Human services at risk.* Lexington, MA: D. C. Heath.

Tambor, M . (1995). Unions. In R. L. Edwards (Ed.-in-Chief), *Encyclopedia of Social Work* (19th ed., Vol. 3, pp. 2418–2426). Washington, DC: NASW Press.

Thyer, B. A. (2001). What is the role of theory in research on social work practice? *Journal of Social Work Education, 37*(1), 9–25.

Tropman, J. E. (1998). Effective group decision making. In R. L. Edwards, J. A. Yankey, & M. A. Altpeter (Eds.), *Skills for effective management of nonprofit organizations* (pp. 244–261). Washington, DC: NASW Press.

Tyson Foods (2003). *Tyson Foods, Inc. and Share Our Strength join forces to fight hunger.* Washington, DC: Independent Sector. Retrieved from http://www.independentsector.org/mission_market/sos.htm on January 12, 2004.

U.S. Department of Housing and Urban Development (2002). *How to become a CHDO: Organizational Structure.* Washington, DC. Retrieved from http://www.hud.gov/offices/cpd/affordablehousing/training/chdo/index.cfm on January 12, 2004.

U.S. Department of Housing and Urban Development (2002). What is the continuum of care, and why is it important? Washington, DC. Retrieved from http://www.hud.gov/offices/cpd/homeless/library/coc/cocguide/index.cfm on January 12, 2004.

United Parcel Service Foundation (1998). *Managing volunteers*. Atlanta, GA: United Parcel Service.

Vargus, I. D. (1980). The minority administrator. In F. D. Perlmutter & S. Slavin (Eds.). *Leadership in social administration* (pp. 216–29). Philadelphia: Temple University Press.

Vnenchak, M., & Cronin, P. K. (2001). Case study: The Family Tree. Retrieved from http://www.ze-thedifference.com/Issue_2/familytree.html on January 12, 2004.

Wald, L. (1915). *The house on Henry Street*. New York: Henry Holt.

Weil, M. (2000). Services for families and children: The changing context and new challenges. In R. J. Patti (Ed.), *The handbook of social welfare management* (pp. 481–510). Thousand Oaks, CA: Sage.

Weinbach, R. W. (1990). *The social worker as manager: Theory and practice*. White Plains, NY: Longman.

Wilson, S. (1980). Values and technology: foundations for practice. In F. D. Perlmutter & S. Slavin (Eds.), *Leadership in social administration* (pp. 105–122). Philadelphia: Temple University Press.

Wineburg, R. (2001). *A limited partnership: The politics of religion, welfare, and social service*. New York: Columbia University Press.

Wolensky, R. P. (1980). Toward a broader conceptualization of volunteerism in disaster. *Journal of Voluntary Action Research, 8*(July–October), 43–50.

Wolverton, B. (2003). Surviving tough times. *The Chronicle of Philanthropy*. Available: http://philanthropy.com/free/articles/v16/i02/02002801.htm. Retrieved June 2, 2004.

Womanspace, Inc. (2002). Our history . Retrieved from http://www.womanspace.org on January 12, 2004.

Woolf, V. (1925). On not knowing Greek. Retrieved from http://www.bartleby.com on January 12, 2004.

Zimmerman, L. I., & Broughton, A. (1999). Assessing, planning, and managing information technology. In R. L. Edwards, J. A. Yankey, & M. A. Altpeter (Eds.), *Skills for effective management of nonprofit organizations* (pp. 325–342). Washington, DC: NASW Press.

Index

About the Authors

Felice Davidson Perlmutter, Ph.D., Professor Emeritus at the School of Social Administration, Temple University, is an active researcher and author in the areas of social work administration, nonprofit organizations, and social policy. She has published 10 books and more than 80 articles in professional journals. Her research has focused on social work administration, welfare reform, social welfare, and progressive social change funds. She has received the Lifetime Achievement Award from the Association for Community Organization and Social Administration (ACOSA) and from the Association for Research on Nonprofit Organizations and Voluntary Action (ARNOVA). She is active on the boards of several nonprofit organizations and serves on the Advisory Board of the National Network for Social Work Managers.

Wendy P. Crook, Ph.D., is Associate Professor in the Florida State University School of Social Work. Following a 14-year career as an administrator in domestic violence and disability service agencies, she studied the social problem of homelessness at Rutgers University. She has presented her research on homelessness, poverty, social work administration, and welfare reform at state, national, and international conferences. She has also provided management consultant services for several countries in the Caribbean while on voluntary missions for the Florida International Volunteer Corps.